MIRACLE
IN THE CAVE

MIRACLE IN THE CAVE

THE 12 LOST BOYS, THEIR COACH, AND THE HEROES WHO RESCUED THEM

LIAM COCHRANE

HarperOne
An Imprint of HarperCollinsPublishers

HarperOne

HarperCollins books may be purchased for educational, business, or sales promotional use. For information, please email the Special Markets Department at SPsales@harpercollins.com.

Originally published as *The Cave* in Australia in 2018 by HarperCollins Australia. For more information about sources and the author's original reporting, see the endnotes in the Australian edition.

FIRST US EDITION PUBLISHED IN 2019

Designed by Yvonne Chan
Maps by Alex Hotchin

Library of Congress Cataloging-in-Publication Data has been applied for.

ISBN 978-0-06-291248-0

19 20 21 22 23 LSC 10 9 8 7 6 5 4 3 2 1

For my family, who let me wander and loved me still

CONTENTS

Author's Note   *ix*

Maps   *xi*

Prologue   1

BEFORE THE CAVE

1. A Ride, an Idea   7

2. The Wild Boars   11

3. The Sleeping Lady   15

4. Entering the Darkness   21

INTO THE CAVE

5. Trapped   27

6. The Search Begins   35

7. SEALs Don't Live in Caves   41

8. A Sense of Direction   53

9. Plan B   65

10. Help Arrives   81

11. Hope and Heart   95

12. Unraveling   111

13. Getting Closer   115

14. "Brilliant"   129

15. Options   141

16. Politics   153

17. The Little Things   165

18. Crunch Time   173

OUT OF THE CAVE

19. Preparations   197

20. Last Words   207

21. D-Day   213

22. Three More Boys   231

23. Five, Six, Seven, Eight   239

24. Closing Window   245

AFTER THE CAVE

25. Sending the Wild Boars Home   259

26. Bittersweet   267

27. Hunting the Wild Boars   275

28. Controversy   285

29. Appeasing the Sleeping Lady   289

Epilogue   295

Acknowledgments   297

About the Author   301

AUTHOR'S NOTE

This book was possible due only to the hard work and passion of the Thai research team involved: Jum (Supattra Vimonsuknopparat), Nat (Nat Sumon), Tin (Boontin Posayanukul), and Am (Am Puchara Sandford). My heartfelt thanks for all your help and friendship.

THAM LUANG

MAE SAI

◉ CHIANG RAI

◉ CHIANG MAI
◉ LAMPHUN

THAILAND

BANGKOK ◉

LAOS

MYANMAR

CAMBODIA

KOH TAO

THUNG YAI

◉ KRABI

Gulf
of
Thailand

KOH LIBONG

N

LOCATION MAP

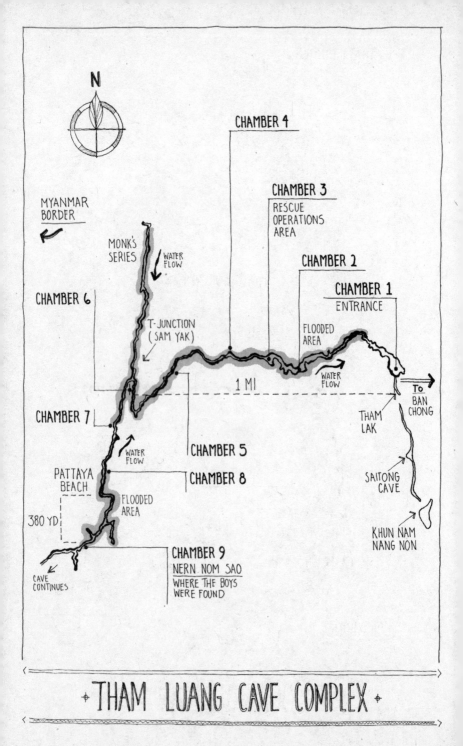

CHAMBER 4

CHAMBER 3
RESCUE
OPERATIONS
AREA

CHAMBER 2

CHAMBER 1
ENTRANCE

MYANMAR
BORDER

MONK'S
SERIES

WATER
FLOW

CHAMBER 6

T-JUNCTION
(SAM YAK)

FLOODED
AREA

WATER
FLOW

1 MI

To
BAN
CHONG

THAM
LAK

CHAMBER 7

SAITONG
CAVE

WATER
FLOW

CHAMBER 5

PATTAYA
BEACH

CHAMBER 8

KHUN NAM
NANG NON

380 YD

FLOODED
AREA

CHAMBER 9
NERN NOM SAO
WHERE THE BOYS
WERE FOUND

CAVE
CONTINUES

N

◦ THAM LUANG CAVE COMPLEX ◦

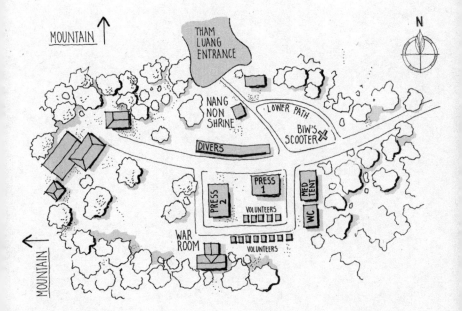

MOUNTAIN ↑

N

THAM LUANG ENTRANCE

NANG NON SHRINE

LOWER PATH

BIW'S SCOOTER ✗

DIVERS

PRESS 1

PRESS 2

MED TENT

WC

VOLUNTEERS

VOLUNTEERS

WAR ROOM

MOUNTAIN ←

STAGING AREA PLAN

PROLOGUE

"Oh, we weren't bored; we were too busy digging."

Fourteen-year-old Biw glanced up. He was sitting cross-legged on a red woven mat. Soft translucent flakes of skin peeled off his feet, the result of more than two weeks in that dank cave. An adolescent fuzz brushed his upper lip—a boy on the edge of manhood, thrust onto the world stage.

He looked around the living room before he went on. About a dozen people had gathered to celebrate Biw's return home with a low-key party. Biw's father, Sak, had invited me to join, along with the ABC's (Australian Broadcasting Corporation's) Thai producer Jum and cameraman David. The family was middle class, with a comfortable house and a pickup truck parked in a carport. But the women still preferred to cook the traditional way—outside, on small charcoal stoves. As we entered, Sak proudly switched on a rather large water feature taking up most of their courtyard. Inside, plates of food were spread out on the floor. The heat of the day had passed, and the tiles were cool in between the woven mats. The family and select friends sat cross-legged, like Biw, sipping beers and soft drinks and fussing over the boy. A brand-new bicycle leaned against the wall.

Biw's real name is Ekkarat Wongsukchan. Thai names are often long and difficult to remember, so most Thais have nicknames. Some derive from baby days (pink, chubby, small), some are aspirational (Benz, Golf), a surprising number are related to food (crab and shrimp are common), and some are just a shortened version, like Biw's dad's name: Adisak "Sak" Wongsukchan. But a considerable number of Thai nicknames can be traced back to a fleeting moment in the hospital, just after the birth, when a nurse asks about a nickname. In Sak's case, his first thought was Leo—his favorite brand of beer. His wife, Khamee, suggested—not unreasonably—that their son might be considered a drunkard from birth. They settled on Biw, the nickname of a good-looking singer who was popular at the time. And so, Ekkarat Wongsukchan became known as "Biw"—which roughly rhymes with "seal."

That evening was the first time Biw had spoken in detail to his family about what had happened inside the cave. Jum, David, and I sat with the other guests on the floor, honored to have been invited to the party. As the only media there, we also felt a bit awkward at being included in such an intimate family occasion. I'd been talking *about* Biw and his mates for days, these boys from the Wild Boars Academy Football Club, joining many on the emotional journey of their rescue. Now here he was, telling us the story firsthand.

Biw didn't need much prompting from his uncles; he was keen to talk. His voice was quiet, but held the room.

"We woke up at 6 a.m. every day because Tee's watch had an

alarm set for 6 a.m. and noon. Those that had strength would dig first, then the second shift would take over."

Little did they know at the time just how deeply trapped inside the cave they were, and how futile their digging was. Their escape route was blocked: two and a half miles of tunnels had been flooded in a sudden monsoonal downpour. Tons of earth and rock surrounded them in every other direction.

Outside, an unprecedented international rescue operation had been under way. The urgent need to get this soccer team safely out of the cave had attracted experts from the United Kingdom, Australia, the United States, China, and across Thailand, as well as an army of volunteers. Millions of people around the world were glued to their TV sets, radios, and phones, anxiously following as hundreds of journalists at the scene reported every development of what would become the greatest rescue in living memory.

But the twelve boys and their coach had no idea about all that. They just didn't want to look like slackers when they were finally found.

"We had to try to get out," said Biw with a grin. "Otherwise when the officials came, they'd think we did nothing."

As he spoke, Biw flicked the middle finger of his right hand into a finger of his left hand over and over—a nervous tic.

"You know, I never asked him these questions. This is the first time I've heard these details," said Sak. "Did you cry inside the cave?" he asked his son tenderly.

Biw shook his head, smiling shyly at the floor. His downcast eyes highlighted thick black lashes.

For all those desperate days, Sak had kept a secret from the other parents: he alone had glimpsed the abyss, and it had frightened him.

"Among the parents I was the only one who went inside the cave," said Sak. "Even as an adult, I was scared."

Sak never let on how he felt to the others, but his experience inside the cave made him brace for the worst. In his mind, the best he could have hoped for was the closure of finding his son's corpse. "I was the only one that thought differently from the other parents. They had hope, but I didn't."

BEFORE
THE CAVE

1

A RIDE, AN IDEA

The road up Tung Mountain was brutally steep.

It was a serious bike ride for the boys of the Wild Boars Academy Football Club—a fourteen-mile climb to a peak around forty-six hundred feet high. The youngest, eleven-year-old Titan (Chanin Wibunrungrueang), was finding it especially tough. But he wasn't far behind the older boys. Even though he'd been cycling only for a year, he was keen. He even had modern cleat shoes that clipped to the pedals for extra power. They were hot pink.

Titan had a cheeky smile and a way of saying things that weren't particularly funny and got a laugh anyway. There was something naturally adorable about him. His nickname came not from the Greek god, as might be expected, considering his Thai name meant "great." He was named after a car. His father was a salesman for Mitsubishi at the time of his birth and was promoting their new product—a 2.5-liter turbo-diesel compact pickup truck built in Thailand, the Triton. And so when a nurse, catching the father off guard, asked him what his newborn son's nickname was to be, he declared: Titan.

Ahead of Titan was fifteen-year-old Night (Phiraphat Somphiangchai), who earlier had turned down his dad's offer of a lift in the car to the starting line, choosing to add an extra eleven-mile workout before the race even started. (Night's father had also been caught off guard at the hospital, and had to come up with a nickname for his newborn son on the fly. Night's older sister had been born during the Water Festival, so was known as Nam—"water." This delivery happened after dark, so the boy became Night.)

Together with the boys on that ride, as always, was their twenty-five-year-old soccer coach, Ekapol Chantawong. It was Coach Ek who had inspired a passion for cycling in his young charges. They joined around sixteen hundred other riders in the Spin to Doi Tung Temple, an event to promote Chiang Rai as a bicycle-friendly province, held on Sunday, June 10, 2018. Some were racing; most were just testing themselves against the punishing gradient.

The first stretch of the winding road was shaded by the forest canopy, but at about the thirty-three-hundred-foot mark, the vegetation changed into thick green jungle. Jurassic-size palms sprang out of the layer of creepers that covered every surface. At intervals along the road, bamboo poles were hung with colorful vertical flags—the *tung* that gave the mountain its name.

The finish line was the temple at the summit: Wat Phra That Doi Tung. Its two golden stupas overlooked a stunning view across the mountains. On a clear day, tourists might glimpse neighboring Laos and Myanmar in the distance. According to Thailand's tourism agency, pilgrims visit the temple because one of the stupas is said to contain the left collarbone of the original Buddha, which is truly remarkable, considering that the holy scripts say Siddhartha Gautama was cremated.

In their blue Lycra cycling tops, the boys slowly huffed their way up into the mountain mist, which thickened at times into drizzle. If they had any energy to take in their surroundings, they might have noticed a small shrine in the forest between the souvenir stalls and the temple. Next to the deities and offerings was a life-size concrete statue of an animal, its snout raised and pointing back down the hill: a wild boar. But chances are they were too exhausted to notice much at all.

Not that they minded. They liked to push themselves beyond the soccer field. Often after training, Coach Ek would take them swimming, cycling, or exploring the mountains around Mae Sai, the northernmost district of Thailand's northernmost province, Chiang Rai, where they lived. A few weeks earlier, they had done another tough ride up Doi Pha Mee (Bear Cliff Mountain). That day, they had all posed for a photo. It looked like they were standing on a raft, but it was actually a bamboo-floored viewing point high in the hills, a light blue sky with cartoon clouds behind them.

This particular subgroup within the Wild Boars formed in the way posses of kids form all over the world—brought together by school, relatives, and shared sporting interests. Six of them went to the same school: Note (Prachak Sutham, thirteen), Tern* (Natthawut Thakhamsai, fourteen), Night, Mix

---

* Natthawut Thakhamsai's nickname is actually spelled by Thais as "Tle." Many Thai words that are translated into English as having an "l" at or near the end of the word are pronounced "n"—"apple" becomes "apen." While some sources have transliterated the nickname as "Dun" or "Tun," I think "Tern" is the closest pronunciation.

(Phaňumat Saengdi, thirteen), Dom (Duangphet Phromthep, thirteen, soccer team captain), and Pong (Somphong Chaiwong, thirteen). Two of the boys—Night and Nick (Phiphat Phothi, fourteen)—were cousins. Adul, pronounced "a-doon" (Adul Sam-on, fourteen), was the only Christian among the rest of the Buddhist boys. Titan was the youngest, but Mark (Mongkhon Bunpiam, thirteen) was physically smaller. The biggest kid of the group was Tee (Phonchai Khamluang, sixteen). The difference between an eleven-year-old and a sixteen-year-old is vast, but these boys were a tight-knit group and spent much of their spare time hanging out together.

In the days after the ride up Tung Mountain, as their jelly legs returned to normal, talk turned to the next challenge.

"Some of the children suggested a trip to Tham Luang for the next week," said Coach Ek. "I'd been in the cave before, [but] some of the children had never been there. They asked to go and I said, 'If we all want to go, yes, no problem, I can lead you there.'"

The outing was no secret. On Wednesday, June 20, Coach Ek announced on his Facebook page that, after a friendly match at 10 a.m. that Saturday, they'd go visit Tham Luang.

There was no official parental permission requested. That's not how things worked in this small community. The parents trusted the young coach. He always made sure their children got home after their post-training activities.

The boys were excited at the prospect of two of their favorite activities: soccer and adventure.

2
THE WILD BOARS

Kamol Chanthapoon was raised by pig farmers, but as a boy he dreamed of playing soccer.

Unfortunately, at that time, Mae Sai didn't have a soccer team, or even a decent playing field. The most Kamol could do was watch games: he told Australian journalist Matt Blomberg that he and his friends would gather around an old television for a weekly one-hour highlights package of English Premier League.

Years later, in 2016, as a grown man, Kamol founded his own soccer team. Originally, he was going to call it Moo (the Pigs), in honor of his agricultural upbringing. But *moo* was a bit too cute, a common nickname for chubby kids. It wasn't quite the vibe Kamol was after, and it would be an easy target for on-field teasing. So it became Moo Pa—the Wild Boars. The club's logo was a sharp-tusked beast with red eyes, front hoof raised, ready to charge.

Everybody who applied to join was welcomed, and the club grew to eighty-four members. There were three teams, divided by age: under 13s, under 15s, and under 19s. There was only one female player: the daughter of senior coach Nopparat Kanthawong. The Wild Boars became a refuge for sports-loving kids who may not have gone to fancy schools or even had official papers; some of the boys from ethnic minorities in Myanmar remained technically stateless.

The coaches worked their young charges hard, taking their training seriously and trying to instill a code of conduct both on and off the field.

"They're fighters," Nopparat "Nop" Kanthawong told me after soccer practice. "They always honor their opponents, [and] they are good sports during the match, however long it takes, no matter what league."

Moments before telling me this, he had been supervising the under 15s squad's stretching session. Coach Nop walked over to a boy who was younger and heavier than the other players, and, almost without even looking, casually draped an arm over his shoulder just as he was about to topple over. It was a telling moment.

Assisting Coach Nop at the Wild Boars was Coach Ek—quiet, fit, and devoutly Buddhist. He had spent his younger years moving between Myanmar, Mae Sai, and Lamphun, almost two hundred miles south, where his aunt lived. When his Burmese (or Myanmar, to use the modern term) parents died, Ek was left in legal limbo. Having lived for years in Thailand, he could have applied for Thai citizenship, but the process was slow and open to corruption. He decided not to bother, although he once applied for a work permit, which automatically cast him as a foreigner. He lived as a monk for ten years at a big temple in Mae Sai, which had a giant black scorpion statue overlooking the Myanmar border.

When he left the monkhood, he turned to his other passion—soccer. In 2016, Ek offered his services at the newly formed club, the Wild Boars. He was in charge of the under 13s team, but his regular after-practice excursions to go cycling, swimming, or exploring made him popular with players of all ages. The boys adored him, and called him "Pee Ek," or Older Brother Ek.

He wasn't the only stateless Wild Boar on the cave excursion. Tee, Mark, and Adul also lived in Thailand without proper papers. Adul's parents had smuggled him across the border from Myanmar when he was just seven, hoping for a better life for their son. They lived in Wa State, a self-governed area of Myanmar once famed for its fierce headhunting tribes, now infamous for producing most of the methamphetamine that floods into Southeast Asia—ice, crystal meth, *yaba*. In the Mekong region, *yaba* is everywhere: little pills of meth and caffeine, cheap and dirty. It allows factory workers, enslaved migrants on fishing boats, and young middle-class partygoers to stay awake, for days sometimes. It is highly addictive and can turn normal people into violent maniacs with superhuman strength.

Adul's parents wanted their son to grow up away from all that. They placed him in the care of a Christian charity in Mae Sai. He boarded there, went to school and to church on Sundays. Adul thrived academically and at sports. Of all his teammates, he had the best grasp of English. Mae Sai's location near the border meant that special "buffer schools" welcomed kids no matter what their backgrounds. Adul's school—Ban Wiang Phan School—was a brightly painted oasis, with passionate teachers who could educate in ten different languages. Here, like at soccer practice, there was little discrimination between those who had Thai citizenship and those who didn't.

Initially the Wild Boar Academy Football Club struggled, as might be expected from a new outfit. But in 2018, they found form: in January the junior team came in second in the competition, while the under 15s came in third in their league. Then in May, the senior team took home the winner's trophy for their division.

This was an impressive feat for a team of battlers from a small town. It caught the attention of the Mae Sai District chief, Somsak Kanakham. He met with the eighty-four members of the Wild Boars club and made them four promises: he'd give them each a certificate of achievement, provide a small financial reward, try to get them playing in more out-of-town competitions, and try to sort out the citizenship issues for those who were stateless, including Coach Ek.

For these boys who dreamed of being soccer stars, it must have felt like anything was possible.

3

THE SLEEPING LADY

If you ask locals in Chiang Rai about Doi Nang Non—the Mountain of the Sleeping Lady—they will tell you the tale of a beautiful princess.

A long time ago, in a kingdom to the north (now Yunnan Province of China), there was a princess who fell in love with a commoner, a stable boy. Their love was forbidden, but the princess didn't care and became pregnant. They ran away, seeking refuge in a cave as the king's men chased after them. When the stable boy went to find food, he was captured by the soldiers and killed.

The princess was so distraught, she took a long ornamental hairpin and stabbed it into her head, killing herself. According to the legend, her fallen body became the mountain, her blood the water that flows through the caves during the wet season.

Princess Nang Non is said to haunt the area still. At various shrines around the entrance, people pray and light candles and incense, hoping to calm the deadly rage of the heartbroken princess.

It's true that, from a distance, the mountain range does roughly trace the silhouette of a pregnant woman lying down. Doi Nang Non is pocked with caves and sinkholes, but the biggest cave system is Tham Luang. In Thai, *tham* means "cave," and *luang* is a word associated with royalty that's difficult to translate into English. "Regal" is close, but not quite right.

A short distance from the Tham Luang entrance is Saitong Cave and, in front of that, Khun Nam Nang Non (Headwaters of the Sleeping Lady), a lovely pond that fills with aqua-blue water. One village elder said that sometimes the water flowing out of the Nang Non series of caves runs red—a phenomenon locals believe to be the menstruation of the Sleeping Lady.

The keeper of stories, Boonma Kabjainai, lives at the foothills of Doi Nang Non. He is a spritely seventy-nine-year-old with an easy smile, who still jogs every day. He also eats two or three homegrown bananas daily, and proudly offered a plate to his guests as we sat down to talk. On the day I visited, an afternoon thunderstorm threatened, and wispy white clouds hung low in the valleys.

Grandfather Boonma first went inside Tham Luang in 1957. Back then he was a teenage novice monk on an outing with about ten other shaved-headed novices. In their orange robes, they picked their way over the rocks and mud. But deep inside, they heard a moaning sound. They were spooked and turned around, hurrying back outside. Later, when they told a senior monk about the sound, he said it was a ghost blocking them from entering.

A few years later, when he was twenty-five, Boonma went in again, this time making it as far as Pattaya Beach, the tongue-in-cheek nickname for the huge cavern where water runs past a sandy slope. Grandfather Boonma said this chamber was a thing of beauty back then. A shaft connecting to the surface allowed light to shine down, illuminating the water in hues of brilliant blue. The aven was still there in 1997, he heard, but was now blocked by debris and soil, casting the chamber into darkness. Just beyond Pattaya Beach, farther into the cave system, he recalled the tunnel led to a spot known as Nern Nom Sao (Mound of the Young Woman's Breasts). The water here was particularly clear and could be drunk, Grandfather Boonma said, likening it to the milk of the mythical goddess.

Grandfather Boonma has no doubt Tham Luang is haunted. But these specters existed on a spectrum of spookiness. It's not as bad as Doi Yatao, he explained to me. That mountain was so terrifying, even toughened hunters dared not spend a night there. All the mountains and caves had ghosts, he said, but Doi Yatao was the worst.

The caves underneath Doi Nang Non have a habit of trapping people. After his stint as a monk, Boonma became village chief, and Tham Luang was part of his jurisdiction. He paused our conversation to go and get a framed newspaper article hanging on the wall, alongside family photos and portraits of Thailand's beloved former king Bhumibol. The article praised his amateur detective work in tracking down two missing Danish tourists. Their rented motor scooter was found outside Saitong Cave, near Tham Luang. The couple had been gone two days. They were found deep inside Saitong Cave, trapped when their flashlight had died. Thanks to Grandfather Boonma, they were rescued alive and well, with a terrifying tale to tell when they went back home.

But the strangest story Grandfather Boonma told that day concerned a friend of his, Nai Kham Devanjai, when he was just twelve years old. The boy went missing near the aqua-blue pond. His family and local officials searched the area thoroughly. For three days they walked around, shouting his name, but there was no sign of him. Then suddenly he appeared, sitting near the spring in front of the cave. The searchers were puzzled: they'd walked past that spot dozens of times. Nai Kham Devanjai said he'd been there the whole time—that he'd seen the search party and heard them shouting his name, but when he shouted back, they couldn't hear him.

The scientific story of Tham Luang's origin is almost as remarkable as the folktale.

Millions of years ago, Chiang Rai was the sea floor. Long after the area drained, volcanic activity pushed lava up along a fault line that almost matches the current Myanmar–Thailand border, forming a north–south mountain range. The west side of the mountain is mostly granite, the cooled remnants of that fiery lava, while the east side is displaced limestone, the compressed remains of ancient sea life: rock made from the bones and shells of the dead. In geology's epic time scales, the Mountain of the Sleeping Lady is half new rock, half old rock; one part formed by fire, the other by water. The Tham Luang system meanders beneath these two worlds.

Though the limestone is seemingly solid rock, tiny unseen gaps between those ancient lives have allowed the drenching monsoons of northern Thailand to soak through. Over time, tiny amounts of decaying organic matter in the soil and air above made the water slightly acidic, eroding these underground fissures into cracks and pockets and ledges and caves. At a rate so slow it's hard to comprehend, the water changed the shape of the stone, carving out a main passageway through the mountain, Tham Luang. Each droplet also carried a minuscule amount of calcite, depositing it in a process of slow-motion sculpting. Over thousands of years, the interior of Tham Luang has become decorated—stalactites hanging and stalagmites growing, creating cathedral-like columns where the two meet. Flowstones like half-finished renderings or wavy curtains frozen in a breath of wind. Sometimes the roof sparkled with cave crystals.

Inside a cave, a dry area is a finished work, and a wet rock is alive.

Deep within, otherworldly creatures evolved. Black crickets burrow under rocks—entirely normal, save for the fact they have no eyes.

These caves are a natural playground for local children—places of daring adventure, teenage first crushes, and escapes into nature. While the grown-ups of Chiang Rai have highways and smartphones and bills to occupy them, their children have the chance to explore freely and carve out their own stories, away from adult supervision.

The boys who made up the Wild Boars faced their challenges, for sure, but they were also lucky to be born in a place of lush green mountains, labyrinthine caves, and rich folklore. A place where—given enough time—oceans become mountains, animals become rocks, and rocks become ghosts.

4

ENTERING THE DARKNESS

On the morning of Saturday, June 23, 2018, two weeks after their ride up Tung Mountain, the boys from the Wild Boar Academy Football Club rode their bikes to Ban Chong soccer field, at the foothills of the Nang Non mountain—all except Biw, who rode his motor scooter because his bike was broken, and Pong, who rode on the seat behind him. They warmed up and played their practice matches—just friendly run-around games, nothing too serious.

After the practice, the boys bought snacks from a local kiosk—grilled pork skewers with sticky rice, potato chips, and soft drinks. They spent quite a lot—about two hundred baht (six dollars)—so the stall owner threw in some bottles of sugary orange-flavored drinks as a bonus. It was far from nutritious, but the boys just wanted some quick energy before their next adventure.

They stood around on the edge of the soccer field and ate the lot.

At about 3 o'clock in the afternoon, still dressed in their soccer uniforms, Coach Ek and ten of the boys cycled from the soccer field to Tham Luang, an easy distance of a little over a mile. Biw again rode his motor scooter with Pong on the back. They parked the scooter at the lower path leading to the cave entrance and walked with the rest of the boys up the path to the cave as the others wheeled their bicycles.

On their left, they passed a small concrete shrine with two blank-faced female shop mannequins wearing silk dresses, inside: a double tribute to the mythical Princess Nang Non. At the statues' plastic feet were candles and incense—peace offerings to the angry spirit.

The boys guided their bikes up another small rise to the cave. They were in high spirits. They made up silly songs. Mix sang, "Today is the day I'm walking into the cave," and the others laughed. Coach Ek, Dom, Tee, and Titan had been inside Tham Luang before, but the others hadn't. They had some rope and flashlights, which they pointed at each other, even though the sun was shining. It was a waste of the batteries, but they didn't care: they planned to be in the cave for an hour or so. Some of them noticed a faded old sign among the vegetation on the cliff wall, yellow paint on a brown board. Titan paused to read the sign, written in both Thai and English:

DANGER!
FROM JULY–NOVEMBER THE CAVE IS FLOODED
NO ENTRY!
FROM HERE ON, NO ENTRY!

Titan thought it over. "That's okay," he decided. It was the end of June. The dangerous period hadn't yet begun. He followed the other boys to the cave entrance.

Jagged gray stalactites overhung the cave mouth like rows of shark teeth, framing a dirt slope beyond. The entrance was huge, the size of a hangar for a medium-size passenger plane. The spiky walls funneled in toward the first narrow passageway. Down the left-hand side, stairs had been cut into the slippery wet dirt.

The boys leaned their bikes and soccer cleats against a handrail at the top and continued on, wearing comfortable slip-on sandals. Most still wore their red soccer tops and shorts. They walked down the steps, still boisterous, shining their flashlights around the limestone walls. They were excited, not scared. This was going to be fun.

As they went deeper into Tham Luang, the light from outside grew dim.

INTO
THE CAVE

5

TRAPPED

As their eyes adjusted to the dark, the boys noticed the passage-way widening to a chamber and saw a solid picnic table about 200 yards from the entrance.

The first 875 yards was an easy walk, the cave floor cemented in places. A sign warning DIFFICULT marked the start of a series of boulder collapses, choke points, and chambers. Farther in they went, the air getting cooler with each step, to Mueang Badan (Underwater City), a semiflooded tunnel with a small air space that required wading through.

The boys ventured on until they reached the T-junction—or Sam Yak (Three Paths), as it's known in Thai. Coach Ek remem-bered it from his previous trip. Then, as now, there was a bit of water pooled at the junction, but not too much. Some of the boys took off their sandals along the way, preferring to pro-ceed barefoot. Tee and Note had left two backpacks near the junction, with bottles of water and phones, intending to collect them on the way back out. Turning left at the junction, they came to a short, muddy slope leading down to a pool of water where they decided to have a contest. The aim was to see who could slide down and stop themselves in time to then leap across the water. Every one of them slid down the muddy slide uncontrollably and plopped into the water, much to the amusement of the others.

They carried on past Thong Fah Cham Long (the Planetarium) and then to the big chamber with a sandy bank, known as Pattaya Beach, which had once been lit by the shaft of light from above. The water Grandfather Boonma recalled as a brilliant blue had gone dark.

Beyond, they passed Nern Nom Sao and eventually reached a passage called Lab Lae (Hidden City), named by someone with a rich imagination who had pictured a small village down here, completely unseen by the topside world. Here they found that the passage was flooded—but there was an air gap, and it looked like they could probably swim through.

"Do we want to go farther?" asked Coach Ek.

The boys were keen to push on. They would earn some serious bragging rights if they could walk right to the end of the cave—about six miles—and scrawl their names on the back wall. But it was already around 4 p.m. and they were about two and a half miles inside Tham Luang. If they were going to swim through the sump, Coach Ek needed to set some guidelines. "We have just one hour to go in, and after that we have to come out. We have to start leaving before 5 p.m., because Titan has a tutoring session."

There was also another reason: it was Night's birthday, and his family was throwing him a party that evening.

"Would you all like to join?" Night asked the group.

Of course they would. Little Titan would have to miss the party because of his lesson, but the others agreed to ride to Night's place together afterward.

The boys readily accepted Coach Ek's proposal, and waded into the water.

All of them could swim and would often go for a dip after soccer practice. But some were more confident in the water than others. As one of the oldest and tallest, Tee volunteered to head into the flooded tunnel and check the depth. It seemed okay—he could touch the bottom—so he called to the others and the group waded into the cold water, some of the smaller boys riding on the backs of the taller ones, arms wrapped around their necks.

They pushed forward, swimming—and walking where they could—until they reached another dry spot. There Coach Ek saw that their path was blocked by mud. He consulted Tee. "Should we go back now?"

Tee thought they should, saying they could try to go farther another time.

"Everyone swam back, hoping to come again in the future," said Coach Ek later.

Making it through the sump, they started walking back, passing Nern Nom Sao and Pattaya Beach. They were almost at the T-junction when, suddenly, Biw shouted, "Pee Ek, there's water!"

What had been a small pool just two hours earlier now filled the passage completely, blocking their way out.

"Are we lost?" one of the boys asked.

"Definitely not," replied Coach Ek. "There is only one way in."

He wanted to check just how stuck they were. They had

some rope, so Ek tied one end around his body. He had Tee, Night, and Adul hold the other end.

"I instructed them that if I pulled the rope twice, to please pull me back—it means I cannot go farther. I dived down and found that the tunnel was full of sand and stone, which blocked our way out," he revealed later.

He gave two tugs on the rope, and the boys heaved him back to safety. There was no way through.

The boys looked at each other.

"I felt afraid," said Mark. "Afraid that if I couldn't go home, my mom would yell at me."

Dom wasn't too fussed. "I thought we would be out soon; Pee Ek would find a way out," he said.

But some of the other boys had to rally themselves. "Get a grip first, then find a way out," thought Tern. "Be cool, don't be frightened."

"*Soo soo nah*," said Mix, using a common Thai expression meaning something like "Fight on" or "Don't give up."

Coach Ek told them they'd have to find another way out.

"How?" asked one of the boys.

He told the team to dig and try to drain the water from the flooded passage. They grabbed rocks and scooped the mud as best they could. The air was cool but not cold—about twenty-three degrees Celsius, or seventy-three degrees Fahrenheit. Not long after they started, they heard whistles—like a soccer referee—and the faint muffled sounds of shouting from the other side of the watery blockage. They shouted back, but they weren't sure if those on the other side could hear.

They dug for a while, but it was no use. The water, sand, and stones had sealed their exit shut, trapping them.

Night had been gone all day, but that was usual for a Saturday. He would play soccer, and then he'd usually go on a bike ride or for a swim somewhere with Coach Ek. He normally returned home around 4 p.m., sometimes later. It was now 5 p.m. Night's parents wondered where he had got to, but they weren't overly worried. An ice-cream cake cooled inside the freezer, with the number sixteen iced on top. For his birthday dinner they'd be having pork, cooked on the sides of a volcano grill, like a Korean barbecue.

As darkness fell, their concern grew. Night's father, Boon (Somboon Kaewwongwan), called Coach Nop, who had no idea where the team had gone after the practice match. Boon and his wife, Supalak Somphiangchai, decided to drive over to Ban Chong soccer field: maybe something had happened to Night's bike and he needed a ride home. It had been raining heavily—perhaps they were waiting for a break in the weather before they rode back.

While they were en route, Coach Nop called them back. He'd spoken to one of the other players and found out twelve kids had gone with Coach Ek to Tham Luang. He was on his way there now. Boon and Supalak immediately headed to the cave as well.

As they drove up the dirt road toward Tham Luang, they saw Biw's scooter parked at the lower path. They met Coach Nop in the parking lot, and together they walked up to the office of the Department of National Parks. But there was nobody around. As they headed back toward the mouth of the cave, they saw three parks officers walking out. One of them was crying.

"I'm so sorry," she sobbed. "I couldn't help them. The water trapped them."

Night's parents and Coach Nop were confused. The rangers explained. They had noticed Biw's scooter, so they had gone up to the cave and seen the bicycles left at the entrance. A heavy rain had started, and they were worried about the possibility of a flood. The parks officers went into the cave as far as the T-junction, but could go no farther. Water blocked the way. They had found some discarded slip-on sandals and a couple of bags. They shouted and blew whistles to attract attention, but heard no reply over the sound of rushing water.

The officers tried to reassure the parents and Coach Nop: "Don't worry. Whenever anyone gets trapped in these caves, they always survive. There's high land, and water to drink."

Reinforcements were called: the village chief and the local volunteer emergency-services organization. From there, the news about the missing soccer team spread quickly.

Coach Nop called Sak, telling him to hurry up and get to Tham Luang. When Sak arrived, the place was already swarming with police and soldiers. He realized that something was seriously wrong. He tried to help with the search for the boys, but the officials wouldn't let him inside the cave. Emotions can be dangerous things in caves.

For other parents, the news came much later. Titan's dad, Tote (Tanawut Wibunrungrueang), was at home when his friend called to say he thought he'd seen Titan's bike on the news. The reporter had said something about kids in a cave. Tote turned on the TV and soon saw for himself the boys' bicycles leaned up in a row against the handrail at the entrance of Tham Luang. His friend was right: one of them was Titan's. He left immediately and arrived at the cave around midnight. As he rushed to the entrance, he paused momentarily to place his palms together and *wai* the shrine (that is, make a prayerful gesture) where the mannequin versions of Princess Nang Non stood with their plastic stares. He then climbed the last rise and surveyed the scene.

The cave mouth was lit up by an industrial light, the sort that might be placed near roadwork at night. A generator hummed. The search had escalated quickly and the entrance had been transformed into a command center. Members of two local rescue organizations were there early: Siam Ruanjai Mae Sai and Sirikorn Chiang Rai Rescue Association. Rescue workers came and went; others stood around.

The chief of Mae Sai District, Somsak Kanakham, arrived around 10 p.m. and took charge. He knew these boys, these local soccer champions. He hadn't yet had time to make good on his promise of recognition, money, opportunities, and citizenship for those who were stateless. He phoned the provincial governor, Narongsak Osottanakorn, who was preparing for bed. Governor Narongsak had been in the role only about a year but had gained a reputation for being an honest and effective leader. He drove from Chiang Rai—an hour away—and arrived about 1 a.m. Dressed in a white shirt tucked into black trousers, he stood in the cave entrance, listening and talking to a group of searchers as they updated him on progress.

At about 4 a.m., the generator went quiet. Tote's spirits lifted. "They must have found them," he thought. But as he watched the searchers file out of the cave, he saw no kids. He was confused: Why were they stopping the search if they hadn't found the boys?

The rescue was just being paused. The diesel generator was fuming out the cave, stinging the eyes of those inside. They needed better equipment and fresh manpower. They'd start again first thing in the morning, now only a couple of hours away.

There was no point in going home. The parents settled in to wait at the cave.

Exhausted from digging, Tee asked Coach Ek if they should perhaps find a place to camp for the night. The Wild Boars walked back through the cave system to the Planetarium, about 650 feet from the T-junction. They decided to sleep there, on the sandy slope. There were no comforts; they simply lay down on the cool ground. A few of the boys had phones. They tried to call their families, but there was no reception deep inside the mountain. Hunger and thirst were starting to affect them. They had no water or food: they'd eaten all their snacks at the soccer field hours earlier.

"At that stage, we were not at all afraid," said Coach Ek. "We thought that the water would go down by the next day. Before going to sleep, I asked everyone to pray to Lord Buddha."

In a low monotone, the boys chanted a well-known Pali-language Buddhist prayer. One by one, they turned off their flashlights—all except for Note, whose flashlight was jammed and wouldn't turn off. They went to sleep with its light reflecting off the calcite crystals on the roof, creating white sparkles that looked to the boys like stars in the night sky.

6
THE SEARCH BEGINS

Caving was a passion that had gripped Englishman Vernon Unsworth since he was sixteen. The pocked karst mountains of Chiang Rai Province were a perfect place for the now sixty-three-year-old: a catalog of barely mapped caves beckoning the avid explorer.

It was not a gentle pursuit. He often returned covered in red welts from squeezing through crevices and bashing into rocks. He loved it.

Vern had moved to Chiang Rai seven years earlier, after meeting his partner, Woranan Ratrawiphakkun, known as Tik. She ran a nail studio called Elegant near the Mae Sai foothills, catering to the students at a nearby university. Tik had no interest in caving at all. She was supportive of Vern's hobby, but preferred to stay above ground. Almost every weekend, she'd send Vern and his regular Thai caving buddy, Lak (Kamol Kunngamkwamdee), off to yet another underground adventure. Lak is a former parks officer who had been drawn into caving via

Vern's passion for exploring the region's underworld. He even had a cave named after him. Tham Lak could be accessed via a crawl space between boulders in the Tham Luang entrance chamber. From there a series of small passages (known as Tham Nang Non) headed south until it opened out into a large complex chamber—Tham Lak. A colony of bats lived there.

Lak Cave is not for the fainthearted, with a chimney to the surface barely wide enough for Lak's lean shoulders. He and Vern probably had the best working knowledge of the labyrinth under the Mountain of the Sleeping Lady of anyone in the area.

Despite the amount of time Vern and Lak had spent exploring, Tham Luang and the caves around it still held many secrets. Vern was often joined by other caving enthusiasts, including Martin Ellis, another British caver who had moved to Thailand. Martin had just published a book called *The Caves of Thailand: Volume 2, Northern Thailand,* a companion volume to his previous work about the caves of eastern Thailand. The new book included a fresh map of the Tham Luang cave complex, updating the previous 1987 French survey. Martin Ellis's map credited Vern as the main source of information and extended the known length of the cave to 10,316 meters (nearly six and a half miles), making it the fourth-longest cave in Thailand.

But Vern suspected it was longer still. For years he'd pushed and pushed until now only about 165 feet separated the end of Lak Cave from Saitong Cave next door. He thought there was a link connecting the two cave systems, but finding that link was tough work.

If Vern and Lak could find a passage linking this cavern to Saitong Cave, it would probably become Thailand's second-longest cave. This was the sort of thing that cavers live for, and

Vern was determined to find the connection—even if it meant taking the risk of exploring the caves alone.

These journeys into the caves by himself were Vern's secret. He knew Tik worried about the dangerous solo missions, with nobody to go to for help if he should fall. So he would tell her a little white lie—that he was off to the office or on an errand.

Of course, Tik quickly worked out what was going on. She knew it was no use trying to stop him, but she had a secret of her own: she had the phone numbers of all the national parks staff stationed outside the various caves. Whenever Vern disappeared on one of his missions, she would do a call-around.

"Is Vern there? Okay, just call me when he comes out safely."

On the night of June 23 and into the morning of June 24, Vern Unsworth's phone rang hot.

The staff from the Department of National Parks were calling him. One of the boys' parents had called Vern, too. But his phone was on silent. When Vern and Tik woke at 6 a.m. that Sunday, there were twenty missed calls.

He called the parks officer back and was brought up to speed: Boys lost in Tham Luang. Get here as soon as possible. Bring a map.

Vern grabbed his caving headlamp, a blue helmet, a heavy orange belt fastened with a big carabiner, and his favorite caving shirt, a long-sleeve fluorescent yellow-green polo shirt. It was laid out already; Vern had been planning a trip to Tham Luang himself that weekend. He didn't bother with a map; the map was in his head.

Vern rushed to the cave, just a fifteen-minute drive from Mae Sai. It was clear from the sodden roads and fields that it had been raining heavily overnight.

"*Nam thuam?*" Vern asked one of the officials, using the Thai for "flooding."

"Yeah" was the answer he received.

"Really?" said Vern, feeling somewhat disbelieving. After all, he'd been planning to go in himself.

Vern and the officials inspected a map, and Vern pointed to the T-junction, throwing his few words of Thai into the conversation to try to ease communication.

"If *nam* [water] there now, we have a problem," said Vern, pulling his fluoro shirt over a dark undershirt. "Where's Lak?"

Lak was ten minutes away. When he arrived, he and Vern walked toward the cave. They paused while Lak lit some incense, motioning for Vern to join him, kneeling in front of the two shop mannequins. The men put their palms together for a moment to pray to Nang Non's spirit.

All around the cave entrance, the boys' parents were conducting similar rituals, placing incense and wreaths of jasmine on the ground.

Then Vern and Lak headed off, past the entrance, through the large open cavern with a big sandy slope about a half mile from the entrance—named Chamber 3 by the rescue team—and on to the T-junction, Sam Yak.

"You could see the water gradually getting higher and higher, working its way to coming out of Sam Yak and . . . down to Chamber 3," said Vern afterward.

He waded into the pool and felt around with his foot, marking the direction of the passage with two notches on the roof. Though the water wasn't up to the roof yet, the experienced caver had a sense that the situation was only going to get worse. Vern was not going any farther and returned to the entrance.

Over the course of the day, he made the trek from the T-junction to the entrance five times. Mostly it was to update those on the outside and call for more equipment and people: there was no way to communicate inside the cave; any message had to be delivered in person. He watched as divers from the volunteer Sirikorn Chiang Rai Rescue Association had a go at descending into the whirlpool at the junction, but their bubbles stayed within view. The torrent was so fierce, Vern worried for their safety.

In an effort to stop the water, Vern asked for sandbags to block the water coming in from Monk's Series—the passage on the right at the T-junction—but it was no use. The powerful torrent pushed the sandbags away. The twenty-five-hundred-foot crawl through the passage at Monk's Series was too tight for a person to turn around in; you could only go forward or wriggle backward, doing what Lak called "ninja turtles"—scraping the mud in front and pushing with your legs, to inch along the rock tube. It was a claustrophobe's worst nightmare. If the boys were in there when the flash flooding hit, they would have stood little chance.

"If they've gone this way, no, they died already," said Vern later that day.

He had noticed that the water coming from Monk's Series was relatively clear, probably flowing in from undiscovered shafts and down the relatively short "ninja turtle" tube. But the water from the left of the T-junction was muddy, the porous limestone of the mountain acting as a sponge for the entire watershed and feeding water through the silty main cave passage like a huge drainpipe. A pump was brought in. But it ran on diesel, and soon noxious fumes were again filling the cave, a haze hanging in the air.

On one of his trips to the front of the cave, where there was phone reception, Vern received a call from his friend Robert Harper in the United Kingdom. Rob was a fellow cave explorer and had just visited Chiang Rai, exploring and mapping the underworld. Vern and Tik had farewelled him the day before the Wild Boars entered the cave. But word had traveled quickly, and Rob was calling to say he knew some British cave-rescue divers who could help if needed. Vern noted down their names and returned to the cave. Back inside, it was a free-for-all, everyone doing whatever they could to find the boys and their coach. Vern worked in the cave until after midnight, but they made no progress against the water that blocked the junction.

For Nick, Sunday morning was a lousy way to start his fifteenth birthday—waking up on the hard dirt, trapped in a cave. In fact, four of the boys had birthdays in late June or early July. Night had already missed his party, and it looked as if Nick might, too.

Night thought about his ice-cream cake, still in the freezer. It was breakfast time, and the boys were hungry. It was hard not to think about pieces of pork sizzling on the side of a volcano grill. Note's flashlight was still jammed, the precious battery draining away.

7

SEALS DON'T
LIVE IN CAVES

On Monday, June 25, well before dawn, the first team of the Naval Special Warfare Command, Royal Thai Fleet, arrived. There were around twenty of them, and they were better known as the Navy SEALs.

Like the American commandos—who helped establish the Thai unit in 1956—they took their name from a rough acronym of where they could operate: sea, air, and land. They were Thailand's most fearsome warriors—supremely fit, highly trained, and dedicated to their often-secret missions. Whereas their command center was on a lovely bit of the Gulf of Thailand, about a two-hour drive from Bangkok, one of their main areas of operation was in the three southernmost provinces, known in security circles as the Deep South. There, Muslim insurgents fought a slow-grind separatist campaign against the mostly Buddhist state, with shootings and bombings most weeks. The SEALs also had men stationed in northern Thailand, who were focused on the Golden Triangle—the region where the borders of Thailand, Laos, and Myanmar meet, and where drugs flow along the Mekong River, along the highways, and along mountainous paths.

Whatever clandestine thing the SEALs were doing that day, they dropped it when the call came in to help. This was no ordinary mission. The personal secretary of King Maha Vajiralongkorn had spoken to the interior minister to pass on the king's concerns and encouragement.

This was big.

The call came late at night—2 a.m., in fact—but the commandos moved fast. By 7 a.m., the SEALs had deployed to Chiang Rai, been briefed on the situation, walked into the cave, and were ready to dive.

The SEALs were tough, driven men, strong swimmers and trained in combat diving. But none of them were cave divers. When they reached the T-junction, the conditions they faced were something completely new: a churning brown pond with basically zero visibility. Everything had to be done by touch. Their standard scuba rigs were clumsy in the confined spaces, with a cumbersome tank protruding from their backs, and air hoses reaching from back to front, that were at risk of getting torn off or becoming tangled. A torrent rushed through the cave with such power that it could rip their masks off if they turned their heads sideways.

The bravery needed to go into that unknown cave system, completely blind and ill-equipped, was extraordinary. Everyone who saw it was impressed. Experienced cave divers would later shake their heads and marvel. There was no question these men were risking their lives.

The main obstruction preventing the divers from getting to the next chamber was just beyond the T-junction. A narrow passage was blocked by mud and debris. Scraping and hacking underwater with shovels and by hand, the SEALs managed to widen the restriction and eventually pushed through. But when they emerged into the big chamber beyond, the boys were nowhere to be seen.

The next restriction was even tougher, and the divers were getting smashed by the oncoming current.

The SEAL team turned back. This time, instead of fighting the surging waters, they were swept by the current down the rocky passageways and spat out at the T-junction.

When forty-two-year-old technical diver Pae (Ruengrit Changkwanyuen) first saw on television that the Thai Navy SEALs were diving in the cave, he knew immediately they were out of their depth.

"Wow," he thought. "They're going to throw their lives away trying to do that."

The giveaway was the back-mounted air tanks the SEALs were using—a standard setup for recreational diving, but ill-suited to what cave divers call "overhead environments."

"Why don't we lend them a hand?" thought Pae. "Or at least get them the right equipment to do the job."

Pae had gone through the usual progression of a passionate diver—from completing his open-water course, to becoming a divemaster, then instructor, and then finally getting into technical diving, exploring wrecks and caves. A new job took him to Florida before he could finish his cave-diving course eight years ago, and once he returned to Thailand, it was hard to find time to get back into it. But he knew many people in the Thai diving community. And he could see there was a problem here that needed solving.

"I didn't even think about the boys," said Pae. "Because I know if the rescue team can get in, they will get to the boys. But we need to provide them with the skills, with the equipment, for them to safely go in and rescue those boys."

He talked about it with his sister, Pichamon Changkwanyuen. Her nickname was Chang, which in Thai means "elephant," an ironic nickname for the petite woman with short hair and fashionable round-rimmed glasses. Chang worked as a personal assistant to a Thai celebrity named Narinthorn Na Bangchang. Pae and Chang started discussing how they might help. Chang wondered how they would get the boys out, if they did indeed reach them inside the cave.

"That's an easy solution: use full-face masks," Pae told her. "Go tell the governor's office that we have that equipment."

He left it at that and went to pick up his daughter from school.

If there's one thing Narinthorn Na Bangchang knew how to do, it was how to harness the media for a cause. Over the years, she had hosted several charity concerts, using her celebrity status to raise money for the Nepal earthquake recovery efforts in 2015, underprivileged communities of conflict-wracked southern Thailand, and other worthy causes.

Ae, as Narinthorn is known to her friends, is a singer, an actress, and the producer of a TV singing contest—a well-known face in Thailand's celebrity-mad entertainment scene, despite now being "too old to do television," she chuckled modestly when I spoke to her. Her social-media avatar has blue hair, tattoos, and a rock-star pout, but in person she is elegantly groomed and friendly.

When I met them, Ae and Chang were a charming double act. They often finished each other's sentences, words overlapping, sometimes swapping back and forth several times during the course of a single thought. Between Ae's celebrity status, Chang's organizational skills, and Pae's cave-diving knowledge, they were sure they could somehow help those poor boys and their coach. Now they just needed to work out whom to tell that to.

Ae hit the phones, calling up friends in the Thai media to see what they knew of the situation. All roads led to the Chiang Rai governor, Narongsak Osottanakorn. But the governor wasn't picking up. From 10 a.m. until 4 p.m. the Monday after the boys vanished, they waited for someone high in the chain in Chiang Rai to give them the green light to do something. Eventually, they got on to a senior official and explained that they could organize proper cave-diving equipment for the SEALs. The official said that was welcome news and asked the three of them—Ae, Chang, and Pae—to fly up from Bangkok. By that time, Ae's calls had attracted the interest of a low-cost airline, which offered them all free flights.

They called Pae around 5 p.m. "Get to the airport," they told him. "We're going to Chiang Rai."

Pae wasn't the only one who thought the Thai Navy SEALs might need some assistance. So, too, did Danish technical diver Ivan Karadzic, who first heard the news around midday on Monday.

He was one thousand miles south of Tham Luang, at a resort in a town called Thung Yai, near the better-known holiday destination of Krabi. While beachgoers and rock climbers headed to Krabi, those wanting to learn cave diving went to Thung Yai, where a series of holes in the limestone had been flooded by a dam more than twenty years ago. Ranging from shallow to more than 650 feet in depth, with reasonable visibility, year-round access, and warm water, these caves were perfect for beginners.

Ivan was helping his friend Paul, a Thai native, teach a cave-diving class. The students were going through a "missing diver" scenario, talking through what to do if one of their party disappeared underwater. During a break, Paul told Ivan about the reports he had seen on Facebook—that there were a few men trapped over three hundred feet inside a flooded cave. (Some of the earliest reports were inaccurate.)

"Paul contacted someone in the Thai government . . . and said, 'Okay, we're here, six divers, we're ready to help, if you need our help,'" recalled Ivan.

About an hour later, word came back: don't worry, we have this covered.

Paul, Ivan, and the students put the situation up north out of their minds as they descended into the milky aqua waters to role-play their own missing-person scenario.

By the time the group returned from their dive, the chatter on Facebook had developed into something resembling the truth: thirteen people missing, deep inside the cave.

Again, Paul got in touch with his government contacts and offered them their help. They told him the Thai Navy SEALs were already on the scene but might need some specialized equipment.

Ivan decided to cut short his working holiday and head back to Koh Tao, where he lived and worked. There were more than sixty dive centers on the island, but only half a dozen focused on technical diving. Ivan did the rounds and gathered up specialist gear.

"I took all the equipment that my company owns, all the specialized equipment—spools, lights, all the things that the common diver won't have—and we sent it to a dive center in Bangkok."

From there, the gear was sent up to help with the search in Chiang Rai.

But still their offers of more direct help were politely declined.

That Monday morning, I was in Bangkok, working my way through an eight-page risk-assessment form, with all the enthusiasm the task deserved. I was heading off the next day to Myanmar for a story about elephant poaching—unless I gained significant weight and tusks overnight, the risk seemed pretty low.

As the Australian Broadcasting Corporation's Southeast Asia correspondent, I often traveled alone and filmed my own stories. But on this assignment to Myanmar, I'd be joined by freelance cameraman David Leland. A Pelican case of video gear, a backpack, and a tripod bag sat ready in the office.

After an hour of next-of-kin and flight details, there was a welcome disruption: a brewing story about a soccer team lost in a cave up north.

I took the information contained in local media reports and the news wires and bashed out some lines, stepping over to our homemade vocal booth to record a "voicer"—a short radio news update less than thirty-five seconds long:

> The local team of twelve players and their coach had finished training on Saturday in the northern province of Chiang Rai . . . when they decided to go and explore a nearby cave. It's believed they may have been trapped by flash flooding. Their bicycles have been found at the mouth of the cave, and rescue workers have found shoes farther inside. Navy SEALs have arrived at the cave to continue the search, as worried parents wait outside.

I unplugged the laptop, slid it into my backpack, switched off the lights, and went home. My commute wasn't far—eighteen steps upstairs to where I lived above the office.

The scream echoed off the rock walls, a blood-curdling cry of anguish and desperation.

"My son, come out. I am waiting for you here," screeched Titan's mom, Tai.

She seemed unsteady on her feet and touched Titan's bike for balance, her shouts quivering through tears. The cavernous entrance was lit by a three-foot-wide halogen globe, and rescue workers who had been busy with equipment and plans now stood and stared. Nearby, Biw's mother, Khamee, cupped her hands around her mouth and yelled into the tunnel, addressing the darkness.

"Biw! Please hurry up and come home. My son, let's come home together."

Sak had other ideas on how to get Biw home. He was determined to join the search for his son. When the call went out for ten volunteers to help, his hand shot up. A soldier helped him tie a traditional Thai sarong diagonally across his chest. Twisted into it were boxes of milk and packets of snacks. Sak's plan was to release these care packages into the water and hope they floated to the boys.

About five of these ten-person search parties headed into the cave. Everyone wore a headlamp. Sak's team had a shovel, a hoe, and a water pump. Sak was in decent shape, stocky, with a penchant for Lycra sports tops. Most weekends he played competitive *sepak takraw*, a cross between hacky sack and volleyball, using a cane ball. But even he found the conditions in the cave tough and, once they got deep inside, frightening.

"It was cold," he recalled later. "I walked to the T-junction and it was difficult to breathe. I wondered, 'How could they get in that far?'"

Sak's team was given a job to do a little over three hundred yards before the T-junction. A stream of water poured out from an inlet about knee high on the cave wall on the right, pooling fast on the ground. They started digging, trying to drain the water away and keep the tunnel open. His white sports shoes were soon covered in mud. Ahead of them, the noise of the water was loud as it flowed in from two directions and collided at the junction, every minute thickening the door that sealed off the rescuers from Pattaya Beach, where they thought the trapped team might be. They dug until they were exhausted and then rested inside the cave, watching the soldiers as they tried to lay a communications line to the entrance. Sak looked up at Vern, who was issuing instructions. Both the British caver and the Thai father had faces so serious they looked almost angry.

As Sak sat there in the mud, his hopes sank. He realized the gravity of the situation—how tough it would be to get through that torrent of water and how inhospitable it was in the cave. The air was thin. He understood that his packages of milk and snacks would never reach the boys: the water was flowing the wrong way. At around 3 p.m., a dejected Sak walked out of the cave and into the rain, starting to mentally prepare himself for the prospect that his son might die.

Inside the cave, at the Planetarium, the Wild Boars kept exploring, trying to find another way out. The boys were hungry. Little Titan felt like he was going to faint. When Night peed, his stomach ached.

Coach Ek felt a responsibility to keep his young players calm. Instead of talking about being stuck, he focused on the hope they'd be out soon.

He delved back to his days as a monk, using prayer and meditation to keep everyone positive. If you feel anxious or uncomfortable, try to meditate, he told the boys.

Each night, they would chant a Thai Buddhist prayer together. It was one the boys all knew: "Bowing to the Triple Gem," which was perhaps the equivalent of the Lord's Prayer for Christians. The prayer honored the man who started Buddhism, as well as its doctrine (the Dhamma) and the Buddhist community (the Sangha). None of the boys understood the ancient language of Pali, of course, but the low-voiced chanting and the familiar ritual were reassuring.

Arahung summa sumbuddho pakava
The perfectly self-enlightened one and blessed one, who has extinguished all suffering

Buddhang Pakawuntung abhivatemi
I bow down before the Awakened, Blessed One
(*bow*)

Savakkatho Pakavata tummo
The Dhamma is well expounded by the Blessed One
(*bow*)

Tummung na-mussami
I pay homage to the Dhamma
(*bow*)

Supatipanno pakavato savaka sung ko
The Sangha of disciples who have practiced well
(*bow*)

Sunkung namami
I bow low before the Sangha
(*bow*)

Namo tassa bhagavto arahato samma sambhudssa
Honor to Him, the Blessed One, the Worthy One, the
  Fully Enlightened
(*repeat three times*)

Adul, however, was Christian. Each night, he asked his own god to get them out of the cave.

But nature had other plans. The rain kept falling. The water kept rising.

8
A SENSE OF DIRECTION

The search mission ramped up quickly. But as each new team arrived, with their own ideas about how to find the Wild Boars, the situation became chaotic.

There were people everywhere, from the top decision makers to gawkers. People walked freely in and out of the national parks office. Parents wailed. Reporters talked into cameras and searched for people to interview.

Governor Narongsak had taken charge of the search efforts, with help from District Chief Somsak Kanakham and senior military officers, but as the size and complexity of the search grew, the whole thing became difficult for local-level officials to manage. One of the problems was the sheer number of people involved. Another issue was hierarchy. The SEALs had their chain of command; the police had another. The teams from the volunteer rescue foundations had their own systems. Add to that people like Vern, who were crucial to the search but didn't fit into the formal system. Everyone arrived with the best of intentions, but inevitably they started pulling in different directions.

In the early days of the search, Governor Narongsak gathered some of the rescuers into a room to give them a blistering talking-to. His voice was only slightly raised, but his demeanor was markedly different from the calm image he presented to the worried public at his twice-daily press conferences. In this moment, he was a soccer coach at halftime, waving a finger in barely controlled fury, disappointed his players weren't giving it their all. He stared down those in the room, steely eyes moving from one to the next.

"Whoever said they don't want to sacrifice for this job, whoever wants to go home to sleep, go ahead, sign your name and get out," he said. "I will not report this at all. But if you want to work today, you have to be ready to work every single minute. You must think of them as your own children."

Some in the room shifted nervously. Most stood frozen to the spot.

"If the head of the group disappears, I will report you," the governor continued. "It doesn't mean you have to be here twenty-four hours; everyone can take turns. But you must have a reliable subordinate on duty at all times, so I don't have to keep my eyes on you all the time."

It's not clear what sparked this outburst, but he was really fired up now: the finger became a fist, then a finger again, pointing skyward.

"We can save all thirteen lives. Or no matter how many lives we can save, every life is precious, just like our own. Today, whoever is not ready, just go home. Whoever doesn't take this seriously, go home. Whoever said, 'I can't do this or that,' just take all your stuff with you and go home."

The chaotic initial search started to get more organized when Thailand's interior minister, General Anupong Paochinda, arrived and quietly, almost imperceptibly, took control on Tuesday, June 26.

General Anupong had the authority to bring all the disparate groups together. As a former chief of the army, he could easily command the SEALs and other military groups. As the interior minister, he had direct control over the police. He was also close to the prime minister, who had succeeded him as chief of the army in 2010. They were both members of the influential "Eastern Tigers" faction of the army, a bond proven during the military coup that ousted the government in 2006. Plus, he spoke English, so he could talk directly with those who would soon be flying in from around the world to help.

"There was a change, for sure," said District Chief Somsak. "You could see that the workflow and delegation was very clear. For me, it helped give a sense of direction."

Many involved in the search-and-rescue effort would later describe General Anupong as one of the most important figures in the operation. His arrival was a turning point, changing it from a well-meaning scramble to a more-coordinated effort. But his style was not to throw his power around. Indeed, few people on the mountain even knew the minister was there. He was not in uniform and had also tried to avoid the media. The general arrived with little fanfare, slipped into the national parks office, and began to listen.

The office had become the nerve center of the search operation, and was quickly dubbed "the war room." It was a simple stone building with a pitched roof and large gable. Inside was a big room, and off to the side a smaller room with an attached toilet. On the walls of the main space were a map and faded posters educating visitors about rocks and caves, and there was a model of the cave system that had been partly destroyed when a tree crashed through the roof in April 2016. The model showed parts of the cave with ominous-sounding names: Go Round Kill, Bone Cave.

General Anupong installed himself in the smaller chamber of the war room and set about learning the shape of this battle. One of the first people he turned to for advice was Vern. The British caver had assessed the situation earlier that morning and saw that the cave was flooding badly. The rain had returned, a steady two-tenths of an inch per hour, its effect intensified by the sponging effect of the limestone mountainside. They were losing ground, the water pushing them farther back toward the entrance.

Later that day, Vern emerged from the cave and went to meet General Anupong. The minister of tourism and sports, Weerasak Kowsurat, was there, too. They asked what Vern thought they should do. He handed them a note he'd already prepared:

> Time is running out!
> 1. Rob Harper
> 2. Rick Stanton MBE
> 3. John Volumthen [sic]
> They're the world's best cave divers
> Please contact them through
> UK EMBASSY ASAP

Minister Weerasak carefully copied out the names on a separate piece of paper. All day it had been difficult to get a mobile data signal from the building, but now, by good luck, there was some coverage. Vern called Rob Harper via video chat, briefed him, and handed the phone to the tourism minister. It was a short conversation. The gist was: How soon can you be at the airport? Within six hours, all three men on the list were in the air, making the long flight from Britain to Bangkok.

While divers like Ivan and Pae are drawn to cave diving for the technical challenge, others come at the sport from another direction. This other tribe starts off as cavers, spending their days covered in mud, crawling through tight spaces, and exploring underground labyrinths—what the British call "potholing" and Americans call "spelunking," the latter term jokingly described by one caver as the sound of a person slipping and falling into the water.

For the two expert cave divers flying to Thailand with Rob Harper, their interest in caving started with Boy Scouts. John Volanthen was a young Scout himself, while for Richard Stanton, it was the envy of seeing a friend go off on a Scouts adventure in a cave that put the idea into his head.

"I'd love to do something like that," he thought.

When young Rick watched a TV program about two divers executing what was then the longest cave dive in the world, he was hooked.

"I just knew [then] that cave diving was for me," he said in a 2007 interview with divernet.com.

To get through muddy sumps in the caves they explored, John and Rick learned to dive. In the early days it was simple gear, just whatever they needed to "push" the cave. "Wet suits, wellies, small cylinders, covered in mud" is how Rick Stanton summed up his early caving days in a lecture to the Royal Geographical Society in 2017.

They accumulated new gear and skills. And if the gear didn't exist, they invented it. John Volanthen, an IT consultant, would later create a device that mapped caves during a dive. They both became members of their local volunteer rescue organization, which linked to the national British Cave Rescue Council.

Their achievements were impressive.

Together they set the record for the deepest UK cave dive, at Wookey Hole in 2004, returning to break their own record the following year. Years of exploring the Pozo Azul cave in northern Spain culminated in an epic fifty-hour push in September 2010, with Dutchman René Houben and another British diver, Jason Mallinson. Their nearly five-and-a-half-mile dive would set the record for the longest cave penetration dive.

And then there were the rescues.

In 2004, Rick was involved in the rescue of a group of British cavers in Mexico. In 2010, Rick and John were called in by the French to try to reach a diver trapped by a silt avalanche within the Dragonnière Gaud cave; after eight days, they recovered his body. The following year, they recovered the body of an Irish cave diver in Galway. Their most recent callout had been to Norway, where two experienced cave divers had died at a depth of around 360 feet. After a reconnaissance dive into the icy waters, John and Rick decided the conditions were too perilous to remove the bodies. (However, friends of the dead divers would later return to make an audacious secret recovery effort, the subject of the documentary *Diving into the Unknown*.)

John and Rick became known internationally as the go-to guys when it came to tricky and dangerous cave rescues.

Both men were used to the less-than-lovely diving conditions in England. Cold, muddy sumps were their thing. And that would come in handy in Tham Luang.

Pae woke around dawn that Tuesday. He hadn't slept particularly well. After arriving at Tham Luang the night before, and getting a briefing and a map from the military commander in charge, he went back to the resort where the SEALs were staying. "Resort" was perhaps misleading. The place was old and unkempt. When he lifted up his pillow, ants had formed a nest underneath. It was a restless night.

Before arriving on the scene, Pae had asked around about Tham Luang, but none of his cave-diving friends had ever heard of it before. There was a good reason for this. Most cave diving is done in caves that remain permanently flooded, allowing the silt to settle and the water to clear. Tham Luang was dry for half the year and then filled with monsoonal rainwater, flowing in a muddy torrent through the mountain. This held little appeal for cave divers. But although Pae couldn't help the SEALs learn more about the terrain, he could still bring his cave-diving expertise to help them navigate it more safely.

He found the commander of the morning shift and explained how he could help, talking the senior SEAL through the concept of side-mounted air tanks that hang off a special harness under the divers' armpits. This gives a more streamlined profile and allows divers to squeeze through narrow "restrictions." He also suggested the idea of pre-positioning spare tanks along the way, so divers could push farther into the cave. The

SEALs had had a gut feeling they'd been close to the boys on Monday; hopefully, with the help of the spare tanks, they would find them today.

"He liked the idea right away and asked me to go in with his team that morning," said Pae.

The forty-two-year-old carried a few of his own spare side-mounted harnesses into the cave. As he walked, he could see marks that he guessed had been made by the boys and their coach—muddy crawl marks where someone had explored a side route, and handprints that suggested someone pressing against the rock wall for balance.

Pae made it past the open cavern of Chamber 3 and almost to the T-junction. At that stage, it was still possible to walk or wade all that way. He gave six SEALs a crash course—Cave Diving 101—and some of them got into the sump. Ever-resourceful, those who didn't have proper gear tied lengths of rope into makeshift side-mount harnesses until the real equipment arrived. Some stuck with their back-mounted tanks. The water had risen overnight, and the searchers had lost ground—whereas the previous night the pool had started just yards from the T-junction, it was now about 330 feet away. That meant extra diving and awful visibility.

Outside, the rain kept falling and water seeped through the rocks, pouring out of the T-junction and pushing them back. Pae estimated that the water level was rising by about four inches an hour. Underwater, the SEALs attacked the second restriction that had stopped them on Monday. That stirred up the mud so much that the divers could see their wrist-mounted dive computers only when they pressed them against their masks. These devices showed the depth, time underwater, and other statistics needed to make decisions about safe diving. The dive team had only thirty air tanks to rotate among themselves—nowhere near enough to pre-position tanks and advance safely.

It was tough, frustrating work. The SEALs and Pae knew they were losing the battle, getting pushed back by the water. They kept going all day, but it was no use. Pae eventually walked out of the cave at 11 p.m., exhausted and disappointed.

While Pae battled the torrents, his sister, Chang, was also busy, her phone ringing constantly.

Celebrity Ae's Facebook posts appealing for equipment were working brilliantly. Whatever she asked for, on behalf of Pae and the SEALs, was pledged within hours, boxed up in Bangkok, and sent up to the cave: side-mount harnesses, lights, carabiners, gloves, helmets, rope. One young man had even called up to say he didn't have any money but he had a truck and volunteered to do the twelve-hour delivery run.

One of the biggest requests was for more tanks and regulators, worth tens of thousands of dollars. And there was a catch. Chang had to explain to would-be donors that they might not get their gear back; it would be too hard to keep track of each piece, and some might get damaged.

Few were deterred. The donations rolled in. One day Ae asked for 200 tanks, and by the very next morning they'd already secured 120.

But not all the calls that Chang received were about equipment. Elderly ladies phoned in crying, sick with worry. "Why haven't they been found yet?" they demanded to know. Some called to say they only had one hundred baht (about three dollars) to spare, but wanted to contribute. Chang explained that they weren't accepting any cash, only equipment. (The Thai government had wisely done the same, trying to avoid scammers.) Some callers offered their opinion on the best plan of action. And some calls were just plain weird, tapping into Thai mysticism, with a twist.

"They believe in[side] the cave, they have the angel [Princess Nang Non] . . . so someone called to tell the children's fathers, every children's father, to [get] naked and walk into the cave," Chang recalled.

Another person told her she should print out big posters of handsome guys and take them into the cave, while chanting certain prayers.

"I know how to stop the rain," offered another caller, explaining a complicated method of planting a lemongrass tree at the cave's entrance to halt the monsoon.

Chang did her best to manage her new role as the nation's unofficial counselor. She wanted to be nice, but also needed to free up the donation hotline. "I said, 'Excuse me, I don't have that much time. Would you please text me [instead]? I promise I'm going to read it.'"

The Wild Boars were starving. But by the fourth day, the gnawing and pangs in their stomachs had grown less severe, the pain of their hunger fading. The boys had heard whistles and shouts on the first night, so they were confident someone was coming to save them. Nonetheless, they continued to search for other ways out.

The Planetarium had provided a sanctuary for the last three nights, constantly lit up and sparkling because of Note's jammed flashlight with its remarkable battery life. But as they watched the water slowly rising up the bank, they weren't sure it would remain a safe place to be. The boys and Coach Ek made a decision to head deeper into the cave complex. After a while, they came to a section of dry tunnel that was noticeably warmer than the rest of the cave. They made their bed there for the night.

The next morning, they reassessed their situation. The tunnel was warm, but the boys weren't keen to stay too long there. The water was still rising. It felt like it was chasing them deeper inside the mountain. They walked farther in, away from the entrance, looking for a safer spot to wait.

Past Pattaya Beach, they came to a steep bank that went back more than twenty yards. The clearance offered by the sloping muddy mound would, they hoped, give them plenty of space, in case the water kept coming. Importantly, there was lots of clean water dripping from the walls. One feature was hard to miss: two rounded white stalactites hung down from the roof, with water running like a tap down their sides. It was these unique formations that gave the chamber its nickname, Nern Nom Sao (Mound of the Young Woman's Breasts).

It didn't take much effort to settle into their new home. Coach Ek dug a "pee hole" in the dirt near the top of the slope, and their renovations were complete. They explored their new site and found that the cave wall at the back was dirt, not rock. This gave them hope that maybe there was something behind it. A secret chamber? A way out?

About a half mile away, on the other side of the waterlocked passages, Vern noticed something.

Where before the water gushed into the T-junction, swirling and splashing in a deafening roar, now it was silent. The pool at the confluence had risen above the feeder passages to the left and right, so the new water was being pushed silently to the bottom, like a hose filling a backyard swimming pool. The only sign of the flow was the steadily rising water level.

Vern Unsworth was not a man given to flowery language, but even he was taken by the shift in the sound and the mood.

"It was quiet," said Vern. "I would even say it was eerie."

9
PLAN B

Rawheen Joanglao looked at the plane in front of him with uncertainty. It was just after noon on Wednesday, June 27, at Hat Yai Airport in Thailand's Deep South. The forty-four-year-old was not scared of heights—he climbed for a living—but he was pretty nervous about this big metal tube that would soon launch him into the sky. It was his first time in an airplane.

"What if something goes wrong with the plane?" he thought. "We'll all be dead."

While the SEALs tackled the crisis head-on, all around Thailand, people were coming up with alternative plans to reach the Wild Boars.

The day before, Rawheen had been relaxing at home with his wife and three children. Libong Island is about as far away from Chiang Rai as possible, while still being in the same country— way down south, off the coast of the tendon of land that connects Thailand to Malaysia. Libong Island is a postcard image of tropical bliss, with crystal-blue water, white sandy beaches, and shady trees. In many places, forest-covered cliffs jutted abruptly upward.

It is these rock formations that provided Rawheen and his friends with a living. Their job was to scale up or rappel down cliffs and caves, collecting the small edible nests built by birds and sell them to the Chinese. The male swiftlets constructed these precious nests with their saliva, adding a bit each day for a month to build up a structure the size and shape of a cupped hand, just big enough for the eggs. The nests are usually an off-white color, but even more valuable are the red "blood" nests.

Birds' nests are a delicacy for the Chinese. They melt the nests into a gelatinous soup, which connoisseurs claim can do anything, from curing asthma to raising libido to improving the complexion of the skin, although lab tests suggest the mixture of ash, protein, and carbohydrates has no real medicinal value whatsoever.

But what mattered to the climbers of Libong Island was that people were prepared to pay big money for these nests. Traders would spend hundreds of dollars for a pound of these bird-spit nests, making the risky rope work worthwhile for Rawheen.

Like most people in Thailand, Rawheen and his fellow climbers had been following the story of the missing soccer team on TV. The island's chief called the men, wondering if they could help in the cave rescue. The climbers had been thinking the same thing. Quickly, they gathered a team of eight to travel up to Tham Luang to see if they could assist. It didn't take long to prepare their equipment: a pair of gloves each, and some very long ropes.

The cliff climbers of Libong Island had no idea about the geography of Chiang Rai, but they had heard about the search for shafts down into the cave. They knew they could rappel as well as anyone in Thailand, their wiry muscles hardened by days hanging hundreds of yards above the ground. But to get up to Chiang Rai to help with the search, they first had to put their lives in the hands of this big silver bird, which would take Rawheen higher than he'd ever been before.

"We were excited and at the same time scared."

When the bird's-nest collectors arrived at Tham Luang later that afternoon, they joined a long queue to register themselves as part of the search effort. But there were hundreds in the line, and it was moving slowly. These were men used to action. They gave up on the registration and headed to the hills. The mountain was crawling with soldiers, volunteer rescue workers, and locals scouring the slopes for shafts that might connect down to the cave. The eight climbers from Libong Island found their first hole and got to work.

Their method was simple. Terrifyingly simple.

"One will stay at the top, while the rest will go down with a single nylon rope . . . one at a time," explained Rawheen.

Apart from a pair of gloves, the men used no safety equipment. If the rope broke or a knot slipped, they would fall and almost certainly die. With their anchorman stationed at the top, the first climber would freestyle rappel until he found a ledge he could stay on. Then he would attach a new rope and shout to the next man, who would climb down farther and find another spot to cling to. The second man would add more rope and shout to the first man, who'd yell up to the top to send another man down. One by one they'd descend until they were all positioned at intervals along their single strand of joined ropes.

"The distance between us is shouting distance," said Rawheen. "We just have to make sure each person above and below us can hear."

Rawheen and his friends found their groove.

"It felt the same; our usual work and this rescue is very much the same. We always do this when we are collecting the birds' nests."

That first day, the climbing team went nearly as deep as one thousand feet down a shaft, but they ran out of rope. Frustrated, they went back to the operation area in front of the cave and tried to find more rope. They couldn't. They felt dispirited.

But the following day, the Libong Island village chief flew up to Chiang Rai and connected the climbers to the SEALs, who gave them more rope. After three days of shouting up and down, the military even gave them radios.

Engineer Suttisak Soralump came at the problem from another angle.

Suttisak knew a fair bit about the underground world of Chiang Rai Province. As president of the Thai Geotechnical Society, he'd been deeply involved in studying the region after it was rocked by an earthquake in 2014, probably the biggest Thailand had ever had. He studied the terrain for landslide risks and dam damage, using his skills as an engineer to peer into the earth and make sense of its powerful energy.

"When I heard about the incident in Chiang Rai, of course it caught my attention," said Suttisak.

But then he heard that a team of highly trained Navy SEALs was on the scene and thought, "Oh, that's great," figuring they'd find the boys and get them out soon. He put it out of his mind and got on with his job teaching at Bangkok's Kasetsart University.

On the morning of Tuesday, June 26, the phone rang. It was a friend from Chiang Rai who worked at the disaster-prevention unit. She said they needed pumps—as many pumps as possible.

Being an academic, Suttisak didn't just have industrial water pumps lying about his house. But he did have links to people who did have that sort of equipment—miners, dam builders, and construction companies. Around 10 a.m., he posted the request for pumps on his Facebook page.

Suttisak set some rules. First, this was a volunteer mission: nobody would be getting paid. And second, the pumps must be delivered to the cave site in Chiang Rai. There would be no help with transport. Time was critical and the deal was: pump on-site or nothing.

Within two hours, he got pledges for twenty pumps, and by 1 p.m.—just three hours after Suttisak posted the request—the first pump arrived at Tham Luang.

After successfully summoning pumps to the search site, Suttisak felt good. He'd done something to help. He returned to his academic duties. It was a busy time. He was deep into the process of writing a book, working his way toward a promotion from associate professor to full professor. But that night, his mind wandered back to the lost boys and their coach, the pumps, and the search.

"There should be a second plan," thought Suttisak. "At that stage, there was no Plan B, there was just one plan: pump the water out and get the kids out from the cave—that's all," he told me later.

Again, he took to Facebook, wondering online whether drilling into the mountain might be an option. The response was huge. His geotechnical engineering friends replied with their opinions. The media started to call him. He'd unwittingly un-leashed a storm and now had to harness its energy.

He called an emergency meeting at the Engineering Institute of Thailand on Wednesday evening to discuss the drilling option properly. About twenty key figures of industry and academia showed up. Suttisak stressed to them the seriousness of what they were talking about. If they said they could help, they had to have the practical capacity to make it happen. And if something went wrong, people would look for someone to blame.

They talked through various drilling scenarios. It was hard to know the right approach. As engineers, they were used to visiting a site, studying the terrain, and ordering the right drill for the job. But this was no time for standard procedures. They made an educated guess and ordered a drill to be moved to the site. The hole wouldn't be very wide, only about five inches—certainly not enough to extract a person. But it might be a useful asset to have. Suttisak booked a ticket to Chiang Rai for the following day.

When he arrived at Tham Luang a few minutes before noon on Thursday, June 28, Suttisak was careful to stay clear of the media. He didn't want news of a possible Plan B getting out yet.

"If I expose my identity at that time, that I have a new way, that is going to give hope to society immediately," he said later. "But we still don't know if this hope [i.e., plan] is going to work or not."

On a more practical level, the plan was still only in Suttisak's head; it hadn't even been pitched to those in charge, much less accepted. The engineer sought out Governor Narongsak: the governor also had a degree in engineering, so Suttisak knew he would understand the various technical aspects. He explained the plan to him, saying a drilling machine was already on its way and would be delivered that evening, while another would arrive the following day.

Though the governor welcomed the idea, final approval would have to come from a higher level. After briefing several military officers, Suttisak was eventually invited to the converted national parks office to give a briefing.

He walked past the grove of camera tripods growing in front of the building, left there to secure a spot for the twice-daily press conferences that were led by Governor Narongsak. Inside, the main room was half filled with people. Some wore fatigues, some overalls, others cheap semitransparent raincoats. In the corner, Ae and Chang sat huddled over their phones, wrangling cave-diving gear. On the other side of the main room, a wooden door led to the smaller room, with space inside for only about fifteen people. A soldier wearing the bulbous black and red helmet of the military police stood guard, keeping the chaos from entering the inner sanctum of the war room.

Suttisak was asked to wait outside with other members of his "drill team," who'd also arrived on-site. They sat on red plastic chairs. An hour went by. Then another. Finally, the door opened and senior commandos filed out. The drill team was ushered in.

Inside was a very senior figure indeed: the interior minister, General Anupong Paochinda. He looked tired. Suttisak got straight to the point.

"I am an engineer; my name is Suttisak Soralump," he began, and sketched out a plan to drill into the side of the mountain.

General Anupong listened carefully. Suttisak could see he was doubtful. The engineer continued explaining the idea and how they proposed to pull it off. Then the questions began—detailed, methodical questions that impressed the country's top technical geologist.

It started with the big picture.

"How do you know where the cave is located?" asked General Anupong.

"How will you drill so deep into the mountain?"

"Where will you place the drilling machine?"

"Is there a risk it could collapse the cave?"

And on it went.

Suttisak explained each point. The risk of a collapse was low. The drill machine arriving later that day would allow them to bore 650 feet, or almost 900 feet if they ordered in more rods to lengthen the drill bit. Exactly where the cave was underground and where they would position their drill were still being evaluated. But they hoped to at least make a hole to a cavity near the main tunnel. Hopefully the porous limestone would connect. That would give them options: they could lower a sensitive microphone to listen for signs of life or perhaps lower in food, if they found the boys.

"Hmm, that's interesting" was the minister's response.

Suttisak sensed an opening. The operation would be made much easier if they could airlift their equipment onto the mountain, he said. All eyes turned to the powerful General Anupong.

"Okay," he said. "We should prepare some helicopters."

He assigned a subordinate to look after the drill team. First priority: get some helicopters over from Lopburi, in central Thailand, to do the heavy lifting. For Suttisak, it was game on.

"That's when, officially, my operation started."

While engineer Suttisak was hiking up and down the mountain looking for a spot to drill an access hole toward the cave where the boys might be sheltering, Thanet Natisri was attacking the problem from below.

On Thursday, June 28, Thanet had woken at around 9 a.m., enjoying a slower morning in Bangkok after a recent busy trip to Myanmar. He'd gone there to offer technical advice about his specialty area: groundwater.

Every year, Thanet left his home in Illinois and traveled back to his homeland, Thailand, to volunteer his expertise tackling a huge but hidden problem. For the last thirty years, Thailand had been using more water than nature could put back into the groundwater system, and the demands from farms and households were only increasing. But little thought had been given to the health of the great subterranean reservoirs that sustained life above, while the plentiful monsoon rains simply ran off into the ocean. In some parts of the country, the reserve had run dry, and there wasn't enough water to drink. In other areas—even far from the coast—the underground aquifers had turned brackish.

Thanet became interested in "groundwater recharge" projects happening in Texas and California, and wondered if the same ideas could work in Thailand. So in 2014, he gathered a team of like-minded experts and formed Groundwater Banks. Their advocacy was starting to gain traction, and successes at a local level led to a national strategy. Now, Thanet's annual missions were focused on capturing the monsoon rains to recharge the groundwater supply.

Around midday, Thanet received a phone call from a staff member of the Chiang Rai local administration. The pumps installed at Tham Luang were not working very well, and every day the water level was rising. Thanet immediately agreed to help.

He called his father-in-law, Veera Vasinvarthana. Veera's company was responsible for surveying and preparing the foundations for many of the high-rise buildings in Bangkok. The sprawling capital was built on a delta swamp, so his firm was adept at large-scale drainage projects. Thanet also called the university academic teams supporting the groundwater-recharge projects and asked them to pull up all the information they had on the geology and hydrology of the area.

"Once we looked at that information, we knew that it's something really serious, it's going to be really hard," said Thanet. "You're dealing with limestone caves, which means there's going to be a lot of cracks." The limestone would sponge up the water across the whole mountainside, and much of it would end up in the main cave.

Thanet and Veera pored over the technical data as they waited at Don Mueang Airport for their afternoon flight to Chiang Rai. After landing, they rushed to the cave area, but once they reached the foothills, their way was blocked by a traffic snarl, the backroads choked with rescue vehicles.

When they finally reached the cave, Thanet saw something that puzzled him: workers had just started drilling a bore hole outside the entrance of Tham Luang in an effort to reach the groundwater below.

"I was just standing there, thinking, 'What good is this?'" recalled Thanet. "This was the high elevation. . . . You're going to drill to about 130 feet before you find water—if you're lucky."

Thanet sought out the head engineer for Chiang Rai Province, who was in charge of the pumping operation. They discussed things for a while before Thanet spoke up.

"I have a better plan."

His plan was to tap into the underground aquifer at an easier access point. If the groundwater was all connected, there was no reason to drill through 130 feet of rock outside Tham Luang. They could go to a lower spot and drain the groundwater from there far more efficiently.

The maps and academic reports he'd collected from the various universities in Bangkok told only part of the story. He needed to know how this watershed really worked. For that, he sought out the wisdom of local residents. They told him of a creek in front of nearby Saitong Cave that disappeared into the ground before they could harness it for their own use.

This suggested to Thanet that the water was seeping quickly down into the groundwater system. It could be a crucial clue.

He found the Thai army commander in charge and put forward his plan: drain the groundwater from the nearby Saitong Cave area as well. If the aquifers *were* connected, then pumping out Saitong Cave would also help drain the groundwater below Tham Luang, giving the surface water a place to go rather than pooling in the cave. It was kind of the opposite of the economic saying that "a rising tide lifts all boats." In Thanet's theory, "a drained aquifer empties all caves."

The army commander agreed to the plan.

As Thanet walked back to the mountain, heading for Saitong Cave, he walked past about fifty drilling rigs standing idle on the side of the road. There were four super pumps, nicknamed *nagas* (dragons) for the shape of their spouts. The dragon pumps were powerful but far too big to get inside the cave. The owners of the super pumps had traveled long distances to help and desperately wanted to get involved after three days of sitting around doing nothing. They immediately agreed to help Thanet pump out groundwater. But there was one major problem: they didn't have permission from those overseeing the search.

"Everyone said we cannot wait, [because] every time we try to get permission, we never hear anything back from the government," said Thanet.

Thanet and Veera knew it would take at least a day to move the heavy equipment into position. Waiting until morning for permission to even start preparing seemed like an impossible frustration.

"We've got no time for this," thought Thanet.

They spoke to a senior soldier, and the decision was made to bypass protocol and get the pumps straight to Saitong Cave.

"We were taking a risk to start [the] operation that night, without letting anyone know . . . [but] we don't have time to waste," said Thanet.

The army commander with them on the ground gave the orders, and soldiers began preparing the site for drilling.

While most saw the Wild Boars as being trapped by water, some Thais felt they were being held by a more mystical force—and it was this mystical force that was the key to their freedom.

On June 22, the day before the Wild Boars ventured into the cave, restaurant owner Nattanuch Prasertongh dreamed that a ghost visited her house. The ghostly woman was dressed in old-style Thai clothes: a long skirt and a band of silk wrapped around her chest, leaving her midriff bare. She didn't speak. But

Nattanuch could see that the hem of her skirt and could tell that her feet were muddy. The chef was disturbed by the dream but didn't know what it could mean. She returned to her seafood restaurant and tried to put it out of her mind.

Five days later—as a full moon shone—Nattanuch had another dream. It was same ghostly figure, still dressed in old-fashioned garb made dirty by mud. But this time, she was inside a cave. And this time, Nattanuch says, the woman spoke:

> In the dream, she said her name was Chao Nang Noi Pin Kham [Little Princess with the Gold Hairpin]. She had long hair down to her knees. She had a shackle around her right ankle. I could see her beauty behind her sorrow and anger. Her eyes were red, I assume, from crying. . . . She was extremely sad.

It was Nang Non, the pregnant princess from the folk legend—the woman whose body was said to be the mountain containing Tham Luang.

"She stood like this," said Nattanuch, throwing her arms out to the sides, palms facing backward, as if holding back a large object.

Behind her, in the darkness, was a group of boys. In a Facebook post that day, Nattanuch wrote:

> In the dream, Princess Nang Non told me that she's been waiting for Kruba for over 300 years to release her. If he didn't come, she wouldn't let the boys out. She was very furious. . . . The boys are staying behind a water curtain or stalactites that form the shape of a curtain. There will be a chimney above the boys. After passing the water curtain, turn right and the boys

should be there. . . . . The princess also said she didn't want
any food or other monks. She had a karmic affair with Kruba
Boonchum.

A "karmic affair" was the euphemistic way Nattanuch described the relationship, but what she meant was that the revered
monk Kruba Boonchum was a reincarnation of Nang Non's
lover, the stable boy who got stabbed to death in the myth.

Kruba Boonchum was known as "the Monk of Three Countries," with devotees from Thailand, Myanmar, and Laos. He was
said to have psychic abilities and other special powers. From a
young age, he'd shown prodigious interest in meditation and
even as a teenager was sought after for his Buddhist sermons. He
was bestowed the rarely given title *kruba* to signify his reputation
as an exceptional teacher. Kruba Boonchum went barefoot, ate
a meager diet of fruit and nuts, and kept almost none of the
money donated to him by his followers.

His meditation exploits were legendary. Every year, during
the rainy season, Kruba Boonchum would retreat for *vassana*, a
period of quiet reflection sometimes explained to outsiders as
Buddhist Lent. He would usually spend those three months in
caves; silent, alone, meditating.

In 2010, he took his solitude even further, undertaking an
extraordinary three-year, three-month, three-day retreat in the
Rajagrha cave in northern Thailand. He didn't speak to anyone.
He would emerge when nobody was around to take the food
offerings his followers left for him at the mouth of the cave and
to respond to spiritual questions written down for him. During
that time, his renown spread. When he emerged, tens of thousands of people had gathered to catch a glimpse of him and—for

the lucky ones—to receive a lock of his now long hair. Kruba Boonchum spent four days with his followers, then returned to a cave for his usual three-month rainy-season *vassana*.

Kruba Boonchum's devotion to meditation, his ethical conduct, and his powerful preaching made him revered. Understandably, Nattanuch's post about this famous monk was divisive. While some believed the story and appealed for Kruba Boonchum's help with the search, others dismissed it as quackery. After all, the timing was a little suspicious. Her post came four days after the boys had gone missing. Everyone knew the story of Nang Non, and Kruba Boonchum was the best-known monk in the area. It would be easy to make up a story like this to gain some attention, maybe even promote her business.

There was no shortage of critics. Nattanuch knew this would be the case and tried to address it in her Facebook post: "This is just my dream. I don't want fame. I have a restaurant and a comfortable life."

Nattanuch had grown used to the spooky forces guiding her. She said that for many years a "dark spirit" had visited her and offered her advice that turned out well. It was this dark spirit who had told her to start selling expensive Alaskan king crabs in her sleepy mountain town of Chiang Dao three years earlier. What seemed like a preposterous idea had somehow become a hit, and now seafood lovers flocked to her restaurant.

But she realized how crazy it must sound to others. No, she laughed, unfortunately the dark spirit never told her what the lottery numbers would be. Or told her where she could find cheaper wholesale prices for Alaskan king crabs.

Two days later, she posted another message, seemingly in response to some of the naysayers:

Let me add something from my perspective. Nang Non princess chose this time because Kruba Boonchum has cut off from the past and doesn't attach to anything in order to go to nirvana. [Meaning he has broken the cycle of reincarnation.] She requested but Kruba Boonchum let go. She had been waiting for him to release her but he never came. When the boys went in the cave, she closed down the cave with water and mud. She desperately wanted to meet Kruba Boonchum even if she had to commit a serious crime/sin. Her sobbing in the dream is still echoing in my eyes. Kruba Boonchum has [to] come. I have told my dream. Nang Non princess, please release the poor boys. I wish her free[dom] from suffering. Please let my dream come true.

The Facebook post was spotted by one of Kruba Boonchum's disciples, setting in motion a part of the cave-rescue story that, though barely noted by the English-language media, was central to many Thais' understanding of what happened to the Wild Boars.

10

HELP ARRIVES

By Wednesday, June 27, the searchers were losing the war against water. A huge downpour began just before dawn, and the water level inside the cave began rising by nearly six inches an hour. The rescuers who had started at the T-junction a few days earlier were now forced back farther and farther, until finally they were at Chamber 3. They'd lost some 550 yards. In military terms, they were in retreat.

Pae realized that as more water entered the cave, more diving would be involved. And for that they'd need to stage tanks throughout the chambers. A lot of tanks. He called in his technical diving instructor from Pattaya—an American, Bruce Konefe. The fifty-seven-year-old was a Michigan native who had learned to dive while stationed in Okinawa, Japan, with the US Marine Corps. He later combined those elements of his life, diving for US and Japanese wartime shipwrecks in the Gulf of Thailand. He'd also discovered and explored twenty-five virgin cave systems in Thailand and the Philippines.

Bruce was experienced at running technical dive missions, having helped as a support diver for world-record attempts at the deepest dives. Few divers would ever see depths of "200m" (just over 650 feet) displayed on their dive computers, but Bruce not only had been to those depths, he had *worked* that far below the surface, on wrecks and in helping other divers.

He arrived at the cave site on Wednesday afternoon and met up with Pae. They entered Tham Luang as far as Chamber 3, where the waterline slowly crept up the big slope of the forward command area. Then they started to work out just how many tanks they would need to pre-position throughout the cave—if they did catch a break and the water stabilized.

Pae's new friends, the SEALs, had installed three submersible pumps. These pumps weren't that big, and there were problems getting a reliable electricity supply to power them. In the end, they managed to get only one working. But it was nowhere near enough. The water kept rising.

There was one success, though. The soldiers found an old wired radio—technology from fifty years ago—and installed a power line between the entrance and Chamber 3, providing crucial communications to the innermost staging area. This by-passed the arduous ninety-minute walk, now at times through neck-deep water, to get messages in and out.

Just before Chamber 3, there was a narrow and twisted sump, like an S-bend in a sink drain. Getting through it in-volved corkscrewing your body around the rocks. As the water rose, the air gap in the S-bend got smaller. Those in Chamber 3 who couldn't dive were sent out. It *may* have been possible to swim through just by holding your breath, but it would have taken nerves of steel, and any snag could quickly turn fatal. By the day's end, it had sealed shut. It was a nuisance for the divers, who had to strap their gear on again. But for non-divers, that short, tricky watery dip was as good as a locked door.

The retreat from Chamber 3 was a serious blow to morale. Things were bad. But reinforcements from all across the globe were quickly descending upon Tham Luang to lend their expertise to the rescue effort.

When the British divers Rick and John, and caver Rob, arrived at Chiang Rai Airport, there was an awkward moment. Someone had made up a banner at the airport—something about them being the best cave divers in the world—and the three were asked to stand in front of it for a photo. They did so reluctantly; it was not the sort of claim these modest men would make, *and* they were wasting time. But they'd just arrived and didn't want to be rude.

They had a briefing at the airport with Governor Narongsak. The divers asked about the weather forecast and whether any of the boys had preexisting medical conditions, and were surprised when they found out that that information was not known. One thing was made clear to them, though: the military was in charge of the diving operation.

There were several government departments involved in getting the British divers to Thailand, and each agency had sent cars to drive the three cave rescue divers to Tham Luang, about forty miles away. So in the end it was a convoy of about ten vehicles that sped down the highway that Wednesday evening. They got to the cave around 8 p.m.

But after flying around the world and racing to the cave, the

British divers were puzzled at finding themselves left to fend for themselves.

"We arrived on-site, and we were abandoned," said John Volanthen. "We had no real introductions, nothing. On that day, it was utter chaos, with people everywhere. . . . We were effectively left to our own devices."

The team found a room to set up as their base of operations, a place for their diving gear. Their first priority was to fill up their cylinders, which had been emptied for the flight. Eventually they managed to borrow a small old compressor. The SEALs "kinda didn't want to help," it seemed to John.

They found Vern, who took them to meet the diving supervisor, a military man stationed in the cave mouth. The entrance was theatrically lit, glowing orange from the yard-wide spherical lamp and other smaller lights. The soccer team's bikes still leaned against the handrail, a powerful reminder of the lives at stake. Below, hundreds of people swarmed around the cavern.

The first meeting between the SEALs and the British experts did not go well. The commandos had been working hard, well beyond their comfort zone, and bristled at the idea that John and Rick, "two middle-aged men" (John's words), could do something they couldn't.

"There was significant tension," said John. "We had no rank, we had no sway. . . . As much as we didn't know how to communicate with the military, they didn't know how to communicate with us, either."

Inside Chamber 3, the water level was now rising about twelve inches every ten minutes. The military had ordered that all diving be suspended due to the dangerous conditions.

"The SEALs team didn't allow them to go in," said Pae. "It was bad enough that the issue escalated up to the Ministry of Foreign Affairs. Eventually, Rear Admiral Arpakorn Yuukong-kaew [the top SEALs commander] said, 'Just let them go.'"

Someone muttered, "If they die in there, don't expect us to retrieve their bodies."

Vern and Rob helped carry the air cylinders in with Rick and John. About a half mile in, they came to an arch followed by a dip that was about waist deep. Rob helped them through the half-filled sump, into the forward operating base the military had set up in Chamber 3. The water was rising visibly up the cave wall, and Rob returned through the rapidly filling S-bend, so he didn't get trapped without diving gear. The SEALs and other Thais inside hurried to clear Chamber 3.

By the time John and Rick got their tanks and masks on, the lowest point had fully flooded. They dived into the sump and laid a line back through as a guide, securing their exit in case conditions worsened. The line, a little over one-tenth of an inch thick, was made of polypropylene material similar to nylon but nonabsorbent, with neutral buoyancy, and would be strong when wet. It was the first in a series of guidelines through the cave that would come to play a crucial role in the diving operation.

"We stopped that night, because it was very clear the cave was flooding," said John.

The British divers emerged after midnight, rejoining Vern and Rob on the other side of the flooded dip. As they walked out, Vern predicted that the cave would flood to the entrance in about four hours. It did exactly that, prompting an urgent evacuation of all people inside the cave.

Earlier, before dawn that Wednesday, Major Charles Hodges got a call from his director of operations. They were stationed on the Okinawa military base, as part of the US Indo-Pacific Command.

"Hey, sir, I'm sure you're tracking that there's a soccer team stuck in a cave in Thailand. Uh, be ready, 'cause we're being notified that we might head out" is how Major Hodges later remembered the conversation to the Australian Broadcasting Corporation's *Four Corners* program.

"Awesome," he thought. "That's exactly the type of mission we want to be called up for."

Major Hodges's Special Tactics Squadron trained mostly for battlefield scenarios, but the prospect of saving civilians, especially children, was highly motivating for these already highly motivated soldiers.

Hours later, a team of around thirty personnel from the Japanese base were loading up an MC-130 transport plane. Many of those deploying were from the US Air Force's 353rd Special Operations Group, trained in personnel-recovery techniques. There was also a survival expert, a cave diver from the 31st Rescue Squadron, and civilian support staff.

The Americans arrived at Tham Luang around 1 a.m. on Thursday and immediately assessed the situation, walking in as far as the floodwaters would allow.

"So we go into the cave, and it was completely dark, and, like, I'm walking in thinking, 'This is so surreal,'" said Captain Jessica Tait, an air force public affairs officer, who would become the face of the US mission over the coming days. "It's so dark. A few of us had headlamps. I did not, so I'm trying to tag along as close as I can to some of the other members of the team. But I could just sense, like, oh my gosh, there's twelve children and a coach in here, and I'm just in the entranceway, and I'm spooked out."

Coach Ek was also starting to get spooked by the grim situation he and the boys found themselves in.

"The most worrying things for us were the darkness, the water, and hunger. The water kept rising all the time. The darkness limited our awareness of whether we could survive in this shelter. Hunger was a big obstacle. When everyone was so hungry, it could cause conflict with each other."

Then a dark thought entered his mind.

"Imagine if all this led to eating your friends, eating your own people."

He laughed at the paranoia that had seeped into the dank cave. It must never come to that. They knew someone was looking for them; they just had to be patient and stay alive.

Just hours after their first dive, the British team dragged their jet-lagged bodies back to the cave around 10 a.m. on Thursday to try again. One thing about their appearance immediately stood out: the inner tube that Rick wore as a buoyancy device. He called it his "lucky wing." It had been part of his gear on several successful rescues and had become something of a lucky talisman, as well as an in-joke. But to anyone who didn't know these cavers, it may have branded them as amateurs. (When another diver saw it, his first thought was: "These guys are going to get themselves killed.")

Cavers are known for using whatever equipment is necessary to push deeper into a cave, not bothered by fancy products or what other people might think. Rick already knew the cave search would not involve great depths, and he and John were used to improvising gear. For years they had strapped doormats to their chests for heat retention in the cold sumps of the United Kingdom. Eventually a dive company borrowed their idea and released a similar product. They had used chest-mounted and side-mounted rebreathers long before the practice became common. These highly technical systems absorbed carbon dioxide from the diver's exhalation and reused the oxygen, allowing longer dives. But a small number of the British cavers operating at John and Rick's level took things even further; they developed rebreathers that could be taken apart and reassembled underwater, in case of a failure. Their technical understanding was top-level, but Rick's rubber ring might not have done them any favors as far as their being taken seriously when they first arrived at Tham Luang.

That morning, though, it was a struggle for Rick and John to even get into the water.

They had already been delayed once when they were asked to move the air compressor they were using to fill up their tanks away from a building in which meetings were being held. They'd just set it up again when it fell silent. It was out of fuel.

It was a frustrating moment. These divers, who had pulled off some of the toughest cave rescues in history, had flown across the world to help, only to be thwarted by a few gallons of gas.

Everyone around them looked busy, and nobody seemed to care. But then a man wearing a yellow name tag—discreetly marking him as a representative of the king—approached to ask if they needed anything. A supply run to a local gas station was arranged. Soon, they had their air compressor rumbling again.

Rick and John finally dived into the first murky pool at around 11 a.m. There were now three separate flooded sections before Chamber 3: a fifty-foot sump; another about thirty feet long; and the S-bend, which now involved about fifteen feet of diving. The water was pulsating, the result of being forced with considerable pressure through narrow passages and into more-open "swirl chambers" like Chamber 3, creating thrumming eddies as it continued to rise.

The British divers surfaced, and in the darkness they saw movement. For a moment they thought they'd found the Wild Boars. But as their lights focused, they were astonished to find four men—Thais from one of the pumping teams. They'd been working in the cave for two days and on Wednesday had decided to take a nap in a quiet corner of the large, sandy chamber.

"When I woke up I thought to myself, 'Why is the cave half flooded?' So I ran out to look toward the entrance," said Surapin Chaichompoo, the president of the Thai Well Water Association, in an interview later. "I looked back and ran to the high mound where we were sleeping. It turned out everyone had left and it was only the four of us left. I told my guys, 'Wake up, wake up.'"

Somehow, in the rushed evacuation, nobody had noticed the missing men. They spent the night inside Chamber 3. They hoped that the water level would go down and they could escape. On Thursday morning, the men heard clanking sounds from the water. Surapin Chaichompoo threw a rock toward the sound, trying to attract attention. The clanking got louder, but there was no human response. So he threw another rock. Then he saw light under the water, and the divers surfaced.

The foreigners were stunned.

"Okay, oh my god," one said, according to Surapin.

The British divers had to temporarily abandon their search for the Wild Boars while they rescued the rescuers. They took it in turns, with the non-diver lending his mask to one of the Thai men, who breathed from a spare mouthpiece attached with a twenty-inch hose to one of the three side-mounted tanks.

"I borrowed Rick's mask," said John. "I put one guy under my arm and then essentially dragged them out through one sump, then returned with my mask, and Rick and I swapped."

The Thais tried to assist, swimming in the right direction, as the British divers held them with one hand while the other hand felt along the line they had installed the previous evening. But any movement by the men was counterproductive.

"We both realized how difficult it was to do that [even] with people who were trying to help, over a short sump," said John.

It took up precious time, but they had no choice: these, too, were lives that needed saving. Bizarrely, the Thai military initially tried to deny the incident, even to the divers who had just experienced it.

"They categorically said, 'That didn't happen,'" recounted John.

It was only when the American military backed the British divers' story and brought over a senior military man to hear the details that the Thai top brass begrudgingly admitted that the impromptu rescue had in fact taken place. For the four members of the pumping team, there was no doubt about the role John and Rick had played.

"I really owe my life to these two divers," said Surapin Chai-chompoo. "You have to understand that these foreigners have a bit of crazy in them. They like to do crazy things. But they are very good at diving."

One of Surapin's colleagues said the close call had a lasting impact.

"If you want me to go up a tree, I'll go up a tree . . . but no caves anymore, they're scary."

While the British divers dragged the four Thais from the flooded cave, thousands of soldiers and volunteers scoured the hillside above, looking for alternative ways in. There were plenty of possibilities. In total they would check more than four hundred sinkholes and caves, seriously exploring twenty-eight of them. Vern and Robert Harper joined the search for a day or two, leaving John and Rick to do the diving while they utilized their caving knowledge. They hiked around but, in the end, decided the chances of finding another way down were slim. They stopped looking and returned to the cave site, but thousands of others carried on.

The surveying of Doi Nang Non Mountain revealed just how much water was being brought from across the watershed and concentrated above Tham Luang. This was working against the efforts of the pumping teams below. Something had to be done. Crews of rescue workers, volunteers, and soldiers began diverting the creeks away from the cave. They dug channels and dammed streams, hauling pipes up the mountain to make artificial drainage systems. It was hot, humid, and rained frequently. Everything had to be carried up the mountain, often by hand. It was a task that was not widely applauded, but, creek by creek, they started to stem the flow.

The international influx continued.

On Friday, June 29, a team of Chinese rescue specialists from the Beijing Peaceland Foundation arrived at Tham Luang. One of those was thirty-six-year-old Li Shuo.

Li Shuo had cut his teeth as a rescue worker during the colossal Sichuan earthquake in May 2008. That earthquake was everything you don't want an earthquake to be: strong, shallow, and in a populated area. More than sixty-nine thousand people died. Almost five million were made homeless. The land buckled and broke, with two hundred thousand landslides and "quake lakes" formed by rivers blocked by debris.

By day, Li Shuo worked for a private contractor that supplied risk assessments for overseas deployments of China's army. He likened the firm to the infamous American contractor Blackwater, which made billions of dollars by supplying modern-day mercenaries in Afghanistan, but stressed that his company provided analysis only, not soldiers.

When disaster struck, he would deploy. He'd gone to Nepal after the massive quake there in 2015, but most of his rescue work had been within China. In a country of 1.4 billion people, there was always someone who needed a helping hand when nature turned nasty.

Li Shuo first heard about the situation in Thailand from messages posted on a group chat for rescue workers on the hugely popular Chinese app WeChat. The Beijing Peaceland Foundation quickly chose six people, plus a team leader, to go and help. Four of them had experience rescuing people from caves, including Li Shuo. He had done one cave rescue in China, but it had involved ropes, not diving. He had done plenty of open-water diving, but never in a cave. Two had done the cave-rescue training, but hadn't put it into play in the real world, with lives on the line.

The six rescue workers and their team leader gathered nearly nine hundred pounds of gear and boarded a plane for Thailand. When they arrived at the cave site late on Friday, it was already dark. Li Shuo was impressed at how organized the scene appeared to be. The other experts were friendly.

But at that stage, Li Shuo wasn't too fussed, thinking this would be "just another rescue."

The very next day, the Australian team was deployed.

It was an overcast day in Canberra that Saturday, but the rain stopped while the Australian airmen loaded up the C-17 Globemaster, a hulking beast of a thing in military gray. Big blue crates of specialist equipment, army camouflage backpacks, and mountaineering carryalls were carried up the back ramp and stacked inside. There was over a thousand pounds of gear to load, but that was nothing for this cargo plane; you could drive a tank onto it if you wanted.

It was a Royal Australian Air Force plane, but its key passengers were members of the Australian Federal Police (AFP)—highly trained men with experience diving in flooded caves and operating in zero-visibility situations. Six of them from the AFP's Special Response Group had been selected for this mission, and there was also an Australian Defence Force member who would join the rescue coordination in Chiang Rai city. Accompanying them was a diplomat who would help coordinate, as well as a specialist psychologist and chaplain, in case the worst happened. While this was a search-and-hopefully-rescue mission, nobody was kidding themselves. Those young boys and their coach had been in the cave for a week now without food. The men getting on that cargo plane knew there was a very real chance their trip to Thailand might involve recovering the bodies of dead kids.

As they walked single file onto the tarmac to board the C-17, a rainbow arched across the sodden sky.

11

HOPE AND HEART

By Wednesday, a few of the boys' parents had decided to take a break from the intensity of the cave site and were waiting at a nearby resort, talking and crying. Early on, doctors had told them not to worry: people could survive for days without food as long as they had water, which the boys did. But it was day five. There was a growing doubt. Were their boys still alive?

"I always thought—and I told my wife this—as long as our son has not been found, or his body has not been found, we still have hope," said Titan's dad, Tote.

Secretly, Sak had lost hope of finding his son alive days earlier, after he had felt the chill of the thin air inside the cave and seen the water rushing in. But he was determined to at least bring Biw's body home for a proper funeral.

For Night's dad, Boon, day five was when his hope started to waver. It was hard not to imagine their weak little bodies wasting away in the darkness. What were they doing? Were they scared? How long could they survive?

The Wild Boars figured it might take two weeks to be rescued. But they were determined to exhaust all options of escaping by themselves. As well as digging the back wall of Nern Nom Sao, they mounted exploration missions through the partly flooded passageways. Even with their flashlights, the geography inside the cave could be confusing.

"The first two days we swam and found three slopes," said Biw. "Then the third and fourth day we went there and there were four slopes. The scenery changed. Every day we made a mark and wrote a date on it, and when we came back we drew an arrow."

Despite their efforts to keep track of days and directions, exploring the cave was mind-bending. Each day, the layout seemed different. Biw said he was walking along a passage he'd explored the day before, when suddenly there was a huge drop-off, straight down, with water below. He was sure it hadn't been there the previous day. Were they taking different routes in the dark? Could the flow of water and mud be shifting the cavescape so much overnight? Or were they just hungry and tired and desperate, and getting disoriented in the darkness?

That day, Wednesday, June 27, the Wild Boars had a meeting to talk about their options.

They could just stay there and hope someone found them in time. Or they could try to go farther into the cave and maybe find a way out. Two of the boys had reached the end of Tham Luang once before, and had heard rumors about an exit there somewhere. But they hadn't seen it. Trying to wade through the next sump and push farther into the cave was a gamble.

"If we find an exit, we will survive," said Coach Ek. "But if we cannot find the exit, that means we are trapped by two sets of doors."

At that moment, they heard the sound of water flowing.

Coach Ek asked the boys to be quiet. He shone his flashlight down to the bottom of the bank. The water was rising quickly. They had no way of knowing it, but a massive downpour had hit the mountain early that morning, and the water was now trickling down through the honeycombed limestone, gathering in the main drainage pipe of Tham Luang. The sump they were considering wading through quickly sealed shut. The decision had been made for them: they were trapped on the slope of Nern Nom Sao.

"In less than an hour, the water rose around three meters [ten feet]. We never heard the sound of rain. After that, it was clear that we couldn't go anywhere. We'd just have to wait until the authorities found us," said the coach later.

But they wouldn't sit idle. They would keep digging.

"We thought that at the back of the cave there was a way out," said Biw, referring to the wall at the top of the slope they were stranded on. "At the back of the mound, we tried to dig our way out. We thought we would see the orange farm, because we knew there was an orange farm there."

Biw was half right. There was indeed an orange orchard on the hillside. But at least five hundred yards of limestone stood between them and that farm. They had no chance of digging their way to it. Even if they'd had jackhammers and shovels and enough food for a year, they still probably couldn't have tunneled out. But digging gave them something to do with their days. And it gave them hope.

Those who felt strong enough would fill their stomachs with water to keep the hunger pangs at bay and head up the slope of Nern Nom Sao to scrape away at the wall with fist-size rocks.

Some of the holes went three or four yards in, said Note later. But they always hit hard rock eventually.

The boys were not fazed, though; they kept at it, working in shifts, digging hole after hole, dreaming of that orange orchard on the outside.

One day, when Dom was digging, he thought he heard the sound of children's voices. This gave them all hope, and they dug with renewed vigor.

By Friday, June 29, the SEALs had their sights set on the T-junction. They wanted to see if the huge outpouring of muddy water had blocked the restrictions they had cleared days earlier. They dived through the flooded sections to Chamber 3. But from there, they could only get another hundred yards farther into the cave before the strong current made diving too dangerous.

Pae and Bruce had called in the help of another friend—a Belgian, Ben Reymenants. He ran Blue Label Diving in Phuket, specializing in technical diving—wrecks, caves, and how to mix gases to sustain life at depths humans were never meant to naturally reach.

Even for experienced diving instructors like Ben, the conditions in the cave were something else entirely.

"There was a whirlpool of caffe latte," he said.

Beyond the whirlpool, the water surged out of a rocky tunnel. Ben got into the water and was immediately hit by the rushing flow, somewhere between a fast-moving river and white-water rapids.

With such strong currents and near-zero visibility, the technical divers had to rethink their strategy. Usually cave divers carry reels and spools of thin cord. They tie on at the start of a dive and at intervals along the way, ensuring they can find their way out. They attach little plastic discs and triangles with their name written on them, known as cookies and arrows, to show who's on the line and which direction they took at any fork in the cave system.

In Tham Luang, there was no need for cookies or arrows: each diver was registered and accounted for, and there were no real navigation choices to make: it was one way in, one way out. But the raging water meant that the standard one-tenth-inch guidelines weren't suitable. They needed a thick, well-secured "pulling line," strong enough for a diver to haul themselves along when swimming became impossible. For this, rock-climbing rope, about as thick as a thumb, was used. If there is one golden rule of cave diving, it's this: never lose the line. Instructors will repeat it over and over: never lose the line. In crystal-clear conditions, divers might just keep the guideline in sight, but in poor visibility they needed to keep a hand on the line at all times. Ben's job was to start laying the thick line from Chamber 3 into the tunnel. "Try dropping to the bottom of the Colorado River and, hand over hand, find your way upstream to the source," said Ben, when asked later to describe the conditions.

There was no chance of swimming against the torrent. Ben inched forward, buffeted this way and that, trying not to bump too hard into the jagged walls and overhangs. In narrow parts of the flooded crawlspace, he got stuck. His dive computer broke. His helmet scratched and battered the wall repeatedly. He managed to lay a little over three hundred feet of line, but eventually the conditions became too much.

"It was beyond my personal limits," said Ben. "All the red

lights went off—can't see, got entangled in a restriction, down currents, broken computer; just too many red flags. And—major thing—there's no guarantee the kids are alive, there's no guarantee they are where [the SEALs] think they are, so it's a double speculation. . . . So you're risking your life for an if, if, if . . ."

He trailed off.

Ben dived and walked back out of the cave, telling the SEALs that it was just too dangerous to push beyond Chamber 3. The SEALs group leader, Captain Anand Surawan, thanked Ben for his advice. But he told his men they would keep trying, despite the risks. They responded with a rousing shout: "HOOYAH!"

Adopted from the US Navy, "hooyah" is both a morale-boosting exclamation and a way to say yes or acknowledge an order. It would become a rallying cry for the mission over the days to come, not just for the SEALs, but for many civilians on the mountain and Thais watching from home. For a few days in Thailand, "hooyah" was everywhere—a way to urge on the rescue workers, the divers, and, most importantly, the twelve boys and Coach Ek still left in the cave.

"The SEALs [have] got the heart, my hat's off to all of them," said Pae. "I'm really impressed with them, because zero visibility, never having the technical [cave] diving skills before . . . and some of them only have fifty dives under their belt, and they jumped into those conditions?! Wow, mentally strong, not just physically. I couldn't speak enough about the SEALs team, how brave they are."

They were tough, too. Ben remembered seeing a SEAL who was carrying an air tank into the cave lose his footing and smash his shin directly onto a rock. Ben winced. The SEAL didn't make a sound. He shouldered his air tank and kept walking.

What the SEALs lacked in cave-diving experience or specialized equipment, they made up for with gritty determination, said Pae. "It's all heart."

Overnight, large quantities of rock-climbing rope had arrived, in different colors. The colors weren't important; they were the only ropes Ae and Chang could get on short notice. The divers needed to lay hundreds of yards of rope through the flooded sumps to get to where they thought the boys might be trapped—at or near Pattaya Beach.

The SEALs devised a clever solution for how to carry the 650-foot lengths of rope underwater without tangles. They carefully coiled them into rice sacks, leaving one end hanging out and sealing the rest of the bag. The rope simply pulled out like a giant string dispenser. Importantly, it was neutrally buoyant in the water. Simple, but effective.

Securing the rope in the cave was a whole other matter, as one diver had found out in the early forays into the cave. He had taken some rope to lay the guideline from Chamber 3. He went slowly, feeling his way forward, tying off the rope every now and then to a rock feature. He'd gone quite a few yards when he emerged into a chamber. However, he was most surprised to see he was back in Chamber 3. Working only by touch, he'd inadvertently looped around the passageway and returned to where he started.

The divers didn't bother removing the loop. Instead Ben found the real passage, and connected another rope with a large rock-climbing carabiner. These clips are rarely used by cave divers because they can be tricky to open with one hand, giving them the nickname "suicide clips." Instead, cave divers prefer the snap clips commonly found on dog leashes. For this purpose, though, the big carabiner was fine—something the divers couldn't miss as they felt their way along the rope. It would, however, make a small cameo in days to come.

When the divers finished their long days, they would walk out of the cave entrance, past the shrine, to the staging area strewn with tanks, gear, and busy people. Beyond this restricted area was another tent city, catering to the needs of everyone who had come to Tham Luang to help.

A small army of volunteers had arrived at the mountain. They came from all over the province and beyond, bringing whatever goods or skills they could offer. Volunteerism is in the blood of Thais. It's encouraged in school, nurtured by Buddhist notions of doing good deeds for spiritual "merit," and it comes to the fore whenever there is a crisis. This was no exception.

Food trucks served hot meals, as did mobile kitchens sent by the palace. Giant vats of curry were stirred with ladles the size of broom stumps. Volunteers stood next to huge coolers filled with water and energy drinks, handing out bottles. There was a sense of festive bustle.

The need was enormous. There were around ten thousand people involved in the operation by this stage, about half of whom depended on the volunteers to keep them fueled. There were four rounds of food daily: breakfast, lunch, dinner, and a midnight meal for those who were working the night shift. In all, the volunteers were producing around twenty thousand meals each day. The food had to be easy to package, hygienic, and nutritious. Sticky rice and barbecue chicken was a popular choice.

There was even a coffee machine—something greatly appreciated by the media in particular, who worked odd hours catering for their audiences in various time zones. It was always busy, serving up espressos and Americanos that rivaled anything available in Bangkok.

The volunteers didn't just provide food and drinks.

Several long tables had been set up offering all kinds of things the rescue teams, media, and families might need, all for free: spare batteries, socks, underwear, painkillers, balms, soap, candies. The thoughtfulness was impressive. Someone had brought a laminator to put plastic wrap around documents and equipment, saving them from the rain. Next to the medical tent, masseuses offered free neck rubs for stressed parents and rescue workers, while hairdressers offered to cut hair.

One day, cameraman David Leland was standing by his tripod near the food trucks, brow furrowed, trying to conceal an inner "meltdown" about some work problem, when an elegantly groomed volunteer in her late fifties walked by and noticed him. She paused and said in perfect English: "Lighten up!" Whatever her precise intentions, the comment *did* make David lighten up, realizing that there were bigger things at stake than his audiovisual dilemma.

The volunteers were coordinated by District Chief Somsak. Whatever he asked for, the answer was always yes. Forty motorbike riders to bring people and goods up the mountain? Done.

While the rescue effort was predominantly male, the volunteers supporting the operation were mostly female. Many wore yellow polo shirts—the color associated with the former king— with blue caps and yellow neckerchiefs. Such was the love for the late King Bhumibol that when his son and successor, King Vajiralongkorn, put out a call for a new brigade of volunteers in 2017, four million Thais signed up. Governor Narongsak incorporated some of this volunteer uniform into his own dress while he led the cave search, often wearing the yellow neckerchief and blue cap. It was a nice touch, signaling that even though he was the boss, he was a man of the people and a loyal servant of the king.

Off-site, more generosity went largely unseen. Hotels, resorts, and village homes opened their doors for the rescue teams, providing accommodation, cooking meals, and washing mud-covered clothes, also for free.

There is no doubt that without the thousands of volunteers, the search for the Wild Boars would have soon collapsed into a hungry, dirty mess.

For engineer Suttisak and his drill team, walking up the side of the mountain was exhausting. That Friday, they were scouring the face of the Sleeping Lady, looking for a suitable spot to park their drill machine.

It had to be just right.

Going directly above the cave and drilling straight down was out of the question. It was simply too far to drill. The cave entrance of Tham Luang was around fifteen hundred feet above sea level, while the ridgeline above rose to some thirty-six hundred feet above the T-junction. Farther along, at the nose of the Sleeping Lady, it was even higher.

Before their trek, Suttisak had asked the SEALs about their trips through the cave. Did the tunnel go up or down? The SEALs said there were rises and dips, but they weren't big. The deepest dive was just under twenty feet. That information, combined with what the engineers knew about the direction the water flowed, suggested that the cave probably stayed roughly horizontal. So there was around two thousand feet of mountain directly above the cave. Although heavy-duty drills can bore almost two-thirds of a mile deep, something that powerful would be too heavy to airlift onto the mountainside.

Suttisak's drill maxed out at just under one thousand feet. So their hole would have to angle in from the side of the Sleeping Lady's right cheek—not too far from where the hairpin that killed her in the legend might have pierced her. The engineers wanted to avoid the layers of hard granite on the lower west side of the mountain and begin drilling just where the softer limestone started.

They hiked up and down the mountain for two days, looking for a place that fulfilled their criteria. It was humid. It was raining. It was muddy. On the second day, some of the American soldiers joined them. Eventually they settled on a spot, but it was all based on guesswork.

"We were quite clear about the topography outside, but inside—nobody knows," said Suttisak. "That's our main problem."

They were relying heavily on Martin Ellis's map of the Tham Luang cave complex, which was hugely helpful, but the engineers estimated a margin of error of between thirty and three hundred feet. (Martin himself urged caution when using his map for the rescue.) Plus, there was no detailed information on the vertical aspect of the cave. So their hole might easily pass above or below their target. It was, to use Governor Narongsak's expression, "like trying to hit a green target in a forest."

However, if their calculations were correct, their five-inch-wide drill bit should hit the cave around Pattaya Beach, where the search efforts were focused. Such a small hole wouldn't provide an escape route, but it might help narrow the search if sounds of life were detected. It might also be useful for dropping in water and food—if the Wild Boars were indeed found alive.

But there was another reason for drilling, something not found in any engineering textbook.

"We imagined that if we were in the dark for six days . . . the thing that we're going to lose is hope," said Suttisak. "So how can we keep the kids hopeful? We'd like to drill to make noise."

Although the drill team thought their hole could be of practical use, they also wanted to make an almighty racket pounding a drill bit through the mountain so the sound would vibrate and echo through the porous limestone. They hoped this would send a message to the Wild Boars, letting them know: we're coming for you.

A mid the constant dripping of water, and the thuds and scrapes of their digging, sometimes the boys did in fact hear sounds. One day, Titan thought he heard a helicopter. Biw heard a rooster crow. Another time, a dog barked: they all heard that one.

Where were the sounds coming from? Were their minds playing tricks on them after so much time in the dark, hungry and scared?

Suttisak was right: some of these sounds did give the boys hope. But other sounds scared them.

"Sometimes we heard people's voices talking [at the bottom of the mound] and we came down, but we did not see anyone there," said Biw.

Even more frightening was the unnerving sound of someone calling their names. It summoned up Thai horror stories of ghosts visiting when people had low energy, unable to defend themselves. "Coach Ek told us that if we hear somebody call our names at night, don't answer," said Biw.

One eerie night, that very thing happened. "I did hear someone call, 'Biw.'"

He didn't dare respond. He just lay in the dark, unmoving.

Barefoot in the mud, Kruba Boonchum formed the center of a moving scrum of people crowding around to catch a glimpse or take a photo. The fifty-three-year-old monk was dressed in dark maroon robes, with a knitted beanie and a walking cane. Upon hearing of Nattanuch's dream, he had come to visit Tham Luang that Friday to try to connect with the angry spirit of the princess Nang Non.

He walked to the cave entrance and performed rituals, lighting candles and incense. He meditated for a while. Many of the parents had a deep reverence for the monk, and watched on as he appealed to the spirits of the mountain—in particular, to the ghost of Nang Non, asking her to open up the cave and let the boys and Coach Ek out.

District Chief Somsak Kanakham was given the job of escorting the esteemed monk to and from Tham Luang that day. As he walked with the monk back from the cave mouth, surrounded by devoted Buddhists and eager journalists, Kruba Boonchum offered him some words of encouragement.

"Don't worry—in a day or two the children will come out," the monk told the official.

The local media caught this, and it spread quickly. Soon every Thai in the country had heard about Kruba Boonchum's prophecy that the Wild Boars would soon be rescued.

The Mae Sai chief was politely skeptical.

"For me, [the prediction] might be guesswork, something to lift the spirits of the people," said Somsak.

If lifting people's spirits *was* the aim, it worked.

When the parents of the Wild Boars heard the prediction, their hope rose once again.

Kruba Boonchum made another visit to Tham Luang the following day, Saturday, but this time it was focused on the rescue workers. A loop of turquoise prayer beads hung around his neck, outside his maroon robes. His feet were bare, as always, and covered in the caramel-colored mud.

"The SEAL divers are not far from the boys," said the monk.

Again, Thais around the nation took great encouragement from his words. But this time, Kruba Boonchum had something tangible to distribute, too: dozens of lucky bracelets. They were red cotton threads with small white beads. In the days to come these red charms would be an immediate sign that the wearer was an inner-circle member of the rescue team, much like a backstage wristband at a concert.

The boss of the Navy SEALs, Rear Admiral Arpakorn Yuukongkaew, took the bracelets for his men. Kruba Boonchum removed a chunky bracelet of big wooden beads from around his own wrist and gave it to Rear Admiral Arpakorn. For most Thais, an object touched by such a revered monk becomes itself spiritually charged, so this was indeed an honor. The navy man slipped the bracelet of wooden beads over his own wrist.

Spiritually deputized, the SEAL commander stood among the air tanks and diving gear as his men lined up. One by one, he tied the red thread around their wrists, passing on the blessing from Kruba Boonchum. But it didn't stop at SEALs. The Australian Federal Police lined up, too, and the Americans. The international and Thai divers took their place. The line stretched out. Each received a red bracelet with white beads.

"It's normal to have a monk who is respected to chant and give mental support to keep on fighting," explained Rear Admiral Arpakorn. "It's like the soldier when they go to war, they need a morale boost. . . . Kruba Boonchum is someone to hold on to. . . . Fighting against nature is something very difficult."

The timing of the monk's gift was excellent. The rain had stopped. The divers were determined to push farther into the cave. Rear Admiral Arpakorn made a rousing speech. Their mission had been blessed and their hands united in this red thread of brotherhood.

"That was a turning point, I think that's the critical point," said the SEAL chief. "I tied this [bracelet] to everyone's wrist and announced: 'Now we will fight.'"

A shout of "HOOYAH" echoed across the mountain.

12
UNRAVELING

While Kruba Boonchum's prediction was reassuring for some, it did little to alleviate the tension of others. The situation was getting more dire by the day, and stress was clearly starting to take a toll.

When the British divers arrived at the cave on Saturday, June 30, to continue diving, they were again blocked by the SEALs. They thought the British divers were arrogant and secretive. This, after all, was their country and their rescue mission.

For Rick, John, and Rob, it was a strange predicament.

"We were brought over by the Ministry of Tourism but were unwanted by the military," said John.

The reason for this schism became clear to them when they saw a diagram of the command structure for the rescue. At the very top was the Thai king, and from there two lines stretched down to military and nonmilitary branches.

The British divers considered leaving. Having seen how fast the cave had flooded, they seriously doubted the soccer team was still alive in there. They had no compressor (the SEALs had taken back the one they were using) and little support. The Americans were also discussing "downsizing their package" and scaling back their operation. Nobody wanted to sit around on a mountainside and do nothing while kids died.

Inside the cave, time was running out, quite literally. Of the three watches the boys and their coach took in with them, only Tee's was still working.

The watch had a date function and had already been programmed to beep at 6 a.m. and midday. The boys left the alarms on so they could keep some kind of routine in the darkness. In the morning, they would fill their bellies with the water running off the stalactites and head up to the top of the slope to dig or to rest. When Tee's watch told them it was night, the boys lay down on the hard dirt to sleep. It wasn't comfortable; they found themselves constantly slipping down the slope. When the boys slept, it was usually in short snatches, before they woke up to rearrange themselves on the angled ground.

But there was something else that kept them awake at night. Or rather, *someone* else.

Even at home, Titan was a restless sleeper. He would sometimes sleepwalk to the toilet. But in the cave, it was worse. He would talk and shout in his sleep, keeping the other boys awake. Sometimes he would even jump up, still asleep. It was annoying for his teammates, but also potentially deadly. If Titan was to wander off in the middle of the night, he might hit his head or fall into the water at the bottom of Nern Nom Sao. So every night, Coach Ek would hold on to Titan, sleeping lightly, always wary that his youngest player might dream himself to death.

After the fourth day, Note's jammed flashlight finally ran out of battery power. From then on, the boys had to contend with the darkness. They still had other flashlights, but they rationed the light, knowing it could be many more days until they were found.

They had never experienced a darkness like the one inside of the cave. It was a profound blackness, almost like a physical substance, oozing around their bodies. After a while, the darkness started to get into the boys' subconscious minds. One night, Dom dreamed he was being chased by a black tiger.

Titan continued to cry out in his sleep, because of his nightmares. One was particularly terrifying:

> I dreamed I was in a hut with all of us, then I saw Pee Ek turn into a warrior, holding a sword and chasing me, trying to slash me. He was Pee Ek at first and then suddenly he turned into someone else . . . with a red magic tattoo. [The other boys] . . . all disappeared and I was alone.

Titan woke up shouting.

Sometimes, the line between sleep and wakefulness was unclear in that darkness. One night, Pong started to stir. At first, the boys didn't know if he was awake or asleep. "He pointed his finger at me and said, 'Aay, aay, aay,'" remembered Biw. "I was lying down next to him and he pointed at me: 'Aay, aay, aay.'"

It was only much later that Pong told the others what he had seen that night: ancient warriors, wearing red pantaloons and brandishing swords. He was terrified. Was his vision drawn from the Nang Non legend? Were these the king's warriors who had chased after Nang Non's lover and killed him? Or were they perhaps Pong's memories of the hit TV series *Love Destiny* that had obsessed Thais that past year, a new spin on a period drama featuring a time traveler going back to ancient Thailand? Either way, Biw said his friends dealt with Pong as teenage boys are wont to do.

"[Pong] pointed at Tee and said, 'Aay, aay, aay.' Tee gave him a hard shove with his foot," recalled Biw, laughing. "Then Pong didn't hallucinate anymore."

As the days dragged on, all of the boys had moments of despair and shed some tears. But Note wept more than the others. He simply didn't think they were going to get out alive. On Sunday, July 1, it was his fifteenth birthday. But there wasn't much to celebrate. They were alive, but time was running out.

After nine days, they were inching closer toward death, their bodies wasting away. Coach Ek had about the same build as the bigger boys. The younger ones were tiny; their cheeks were hollow, their skin gray. With no food to turn into energy, their normal chemical processes slowed and then shifted, their bodies ingeniously rearranging themselves to seek sustenance elsewhere. The protein in their muscles was broken down into glucose; their fat turned into fatty acids and ketone. Their bodies were consuming them from the inside, fueling the life-giving fundamentals. The heart must keep pumping blood. The brain must keep thinking. They must stay calm, conserve their energy. They must survive.

13

GETTING CLOSER

By Sunday, July 1, it looked like the rescue mission might have caught a lucky break. The weather was easing. There'd been no substantial rain for the last thirty-six hours. Thanet's groundwater team made the most of the opportunity.

Outside Saitong Cave, a drill bored fifty feet down and pierced into the underground aquifer, sending water shooting six and a half feet into the air. That pressure was a good sign for Thanet. It suggested the water was seeping down from the cave system, filling the groundwater space to bursting, and forcing the rest of the water to stay at the surface, inundating the cave. If they could reduce the amount of groundwater, the surface water would be able to soak down through the limestone into the aquifer. That was the theory anyway.

They started the super pumps. Water gushed from the dragons' mouths. It was hard to say exactly what would work: the hydrology of the cave system was complicated, and they didn't have time to figure it out exactly. So they pumped from everywhere.

Some sucked water from directly inside Tham Luang, trying to drain the passage and regain access to Chamber 3, while another pump placed outside the entrance to Tham Luang also tried to lower the groundwater. At full power, each dragon pump could drain 14.8 million gallons an hour—enough to fill more than two Olympic-size swimming pools.

But all this water had to go somewhere, as rice farmer Mae Bua Chaicheun soon found out.

Rice farming is painstaking work. Mae Bua had spent long days shin deep in paddy water, reaching down to place rice seedlings into the mud. One at a time, row upon row, bent double for hours on end, feet wet for days. It was lonely work for her. She was a widow, and her children had no interest in the labor-intensive job of rice farming.

She had just finished transplanting her seedlings from their nursery to the open paddy when she heard about the boys trapped in the cave, just up the hill. She volunteered to help and spent the next five days near the cave entrance, cooking food to feed the rescue workers, the media, and those pumping millions of gallons of water from the cave.

When she finally came down from the mountain, she saw where all that water had gone. Her five acres of fields were inundated by nearly two feet of water, the baby rice plants long dead. And it wasn't just her field; a hundred other farmers also had had their crops destroyed.

But most welcomed the damage, if it meant saving the boys.

"It doesn't matter," Mae Bua said. "I just want the children to get out alive. Children are more important than rice. The rice can always regrow. But we can't regrow the children."

The farmers' sacrifice was worth it. By Sunday afternoon,

the battle against the water in the cave began to shift. Yellow measuring sticks set up at various points within Tham Luang started to show the water level dropping. The lack of rain also certainly helped. A colonel called Thanet to inform him that with the conditions in Tham Luang improving, the SEALs were going back in.

By Sunday, the resolve of the SEAL divers was hardening. The cave was still flooded, but the water flow was becoming more manageable, and the torrents weren't as strong. Behind the scenes, Ae and Chang had been steadily bringing supplies in, and there were now enough cylinders and diving gear to make a big push beyond the T-junction.

That day, the SEALs were determined to lay their guide rope to the T-junction and see how much farther they could go. They were working closely with the team of diving instructors, which by now had a few more members.

Ben had invited Maksym Polejaka, a Ukrainian-born former commando who had served in the French Foreign Legion, and Vsevolod Korobov, another Ukrainian technical diver based in Thailand, to come and help at Tham Luang. Two other divers had turned up of their own accord: Israeli Rafael Aroush and his son Shlomi. The pair had driven from their home in Udon Thani on Thursday to see if they could help and now joined the other foreign volunteer divers.

Together with Pae and his diving instructor, Bruce, these Thai-based volunteer divers were the earliest makings of what would come to be known as the Euro team. In fact, the Euro team would eventually include divers from Canada and Ukraine, as well as Thailand, but the "Euro" tag stuck and was a way to differentiate them from the US and British teams. The Euro team worked closely with the Thai Navy SEALs, who gave the foreigners dark blue long-sleeve T-shirts to wear, with ROYAL THAI NAVY printed on the back.

With the arrival of these experts, Pae took on a slightly different role as dive supervisor and interpreter. Not only did he have to translate between Thai and English, but also between highly technical cave-diving jargon and the language of regular scuba divers like the SEALs. Bruce also stayed out of the water, to help coordinate.

In terms of where they thought the Wild Boars might be located, Pattaya Beach was still the hot favorite, because of the muddy handprints and crawl marks the SEALs had spotted during their first couple of days. But it was still just an educated guess.

The SEALs and the Euro team started work around 3 a.m. on Sunday and slogged on throughout the morning. They dived through the sump, tying the thick guide rope to stalactites or rocks as they went.

That afternoon, the British divers John and Rick made more solid progress, laying more line and coming to an old rope that had obviously been in place for a while, something to help tourists get through Tham Luang in the dry season. Now, with the tunnel full of rushing water, the British divers used the tourist line to inch forward. Visibility was poor; often the first they knew about an object was when they bumped into it. The men were bracing for the worst, and diving blind made them constantly on edge.

"I found—twice—a flexible hose floating in the passage, and I shouted back to Rick, 'There's something in the water,' that I was fully prepared to be a body," said John later.

John and Rick had tried to commit to memory the map of the cave, and checked their progress with compasses they carried. In particular, they were looking for a sharp right-hand turn, which would mean they were approaching the T-junction. (This tight turn would become Chamber 6, but for now it was completely flooded.) Upon finding it, they made the hook right and swam on.

Eventually, John came to a section he recognized from Vern's description: a warm, clear gush of water was coming in from the right—where the water had flowed down the short Monk's Series tube, not for long enough to cool or pick up much sediment. From the left, the water was cooler and muddy from a long journey through the big passageways of Tham Luang.

They had battled their way back to the T-junction.

While the divers advanced inside the cave, Suttisak's drill plans were yet to get off the ground. At a hastily fashioned helipad not far from the cave site, an Mi-17 military transport helicopter sat waiting.

Suttisak and his drill team had chosen the spot on the mountain where they would position their rig. But before any drilling could begin, they needed to create a flat area to work from. To do that, they required an excavator, but the problem was the excavator's weight. The pilot told Suttisak that the maximum weight that the helicopter could safely lift was just over three tons. This was going to be a challenge: most common excavators weighed over twenty tons. So the engineers immediately sent word out to their buddies in the construction business: we need a baby digger.

Soon, a tiny excavator arrived. Its operator looked confused.

All he knew was that his boss had ordered him to go and help someone. It wasn't until he arrived that he found out he and his digger would be lifted by a helicopter onto the side of a mountain to assist a search mission being watched around the world.

An hour later, the drill team bowed their heads and squinted their eyes as the helicopter's rotors churned up dust and vegetation. When they looked up, the baby digger dangled from a long cable, silhouetted against the deep blue sky. The perfectly proportioned miniature excavator made the helicopter above it look surreally large.

By Monday, they had managed to create a flat ledge and put the drilling machine in place. The drilling machine was relatively lightweight and had been easy for the military chopper to lift up and fly around the mountain. But the air pump was still to come and it was the heaviest part of the rig. It needed to be powerful enough to blow the particles of smashed rock back through the inside of the thousand feet of drilling rods. This one was a thousand pounds over the pilot's three-ton limit.

The engineers stood back and looked at it.

There was no other option; they had to somehow turn this three-and-a-half-ton air pump into a three-ton pump. So they began to take it apart, starting with the wheels: they wouldn't be needed on the mountainside. Their wrenches tore off chunks like sharks feeding at a whale carcass. They desperately wanted to get all the equipment in place before dark. The helicopter could fly only during the day, and it was already late afternoon. Once the equipment was there, they could light up the area and work around the clock. But if they didn't get the air pump up now, their whole operation would be delayed by twelve hours.

As the air pump was being stripped, they started getting the drilling rods in place. These also proved tricky, but for a different reason: they were too delicate to airlift. The ends of each rod had to connect perfectly, since any fault could twist the drill bit, with potentially dangerous consequences for those working on it. So these, they decided, would have to be carried by hand up the mountain. Each rod was about five feet long and weighed about forty-five pounds. One by one, the rods were placed across the shoulders of fit men—some soldiers, some volunteers—who marched off along the path and disappeared into the misty green jungle. They were given strict instructions not to put their heavy loads down until they reached the drill site.

Back at the helipad, the engineers finally had the pump down to the right weight. The helicopter took off carefully. The block-shaped air pump stayed stable and it, too, was carried to the drill site.

Soon after, the chopper returned. Suttisak and a member of Thailand's special forces got in and were flown around the mountain to the west side. It was so close to the Myanmar border that when Suttisak waved to the border guards on the other side, they waved back. The chopper hovered over the drill site, careful not to stray into an international incident, as the two men checked their helmets and harnesses and climbed into an orange basket. Sitting with their knees to their chests, they were lowered down.

It was time to drill.

The arm of the drill machine was tilted to sixty-eight degrees, angling into what would look from afar like Princess Nang Non's right cheek. The first rod was loaded into the machine and the power switched on. It roared into life, pulsing the drill rod back and forth. Knobs of hardened steel on the tip of the drill pulverized the limestone. The air pump forced the ground rock out. When the hole reached the length of the rod, the machines stopped while the drillers connected another rod.

Suttisak's Plan B was under way.

A cloud of fine white dust crept eerily around the drillers, who turned their backs and covered their faces as best they could. It looked like a heavy mist, created not by clouds but from deep within the mountain itself.

That Sunday, I was home in Bangkok, enjoying playing through my beloved guitar collection. It was good to be back: cameraman David Leland and I had just spent four days filming elephants and interviews in Myanmar.

I hadn't thought much about the cave story since filing that first voicer almost a week earlier. It was front-page news in Thailand, but I'd been away and busy. Later that day, my boss called to discuss the boys in the cave. He was keen for me to travel to Chiang Rai Province. I called David to see if he was available. He was. The ABC's office manager booked our flights there for the next morning, as well as a few days' accommodation.

I headed downstairs to file a couple of voicers for Monday's morning bulletins. There was some fresh news: the Australian contingent had just arrived.

I repacked the video gear. We'd also be joined by the ABC's Thai producer Supattra Vimonsuknopparat, aka Jum. Her role would be to arrange interviews and translate.

I threw a bag of still-unwashed clothes back in my suitcase and somewhat reluctantly put the guitars back on the rack.

Walking off the plane at Chiang Rai airport the next day, I noticed two guys who looked like they might have something to do with the rescue. I struck up a quick conversation with one, a surfy-looking guy with long sun-bleached hair and a beard. His name was Erik Brown. He told me that he and his friend Ivan Karadzic were divers from Koh Tao, there to lend a hand.

"What are you going to do?" I asked.

"Whatever's needed. Move gear, fill tanks, whatever we can do to help," said Erik, in a Canadian accent. "See you up there."

Jum, David, and I loaded our bags into the waiting minivan and headed straight for the mountain. At the foot of the hill, we learned the shuttle routine. Because of previous traffic congestion, all media had to climb into a *songtaew* (a pickup truck with the bed covered and bench seats along each side) that would take us to another drop-off point. From here, it was a 500-yard walk up a dirt road to the staging area outside Tham Luang.

Most of the walk was a gentle incline, with green fields on either side and a clear rivulet running along one shoulder. The source of the water soon became apparent as we walked on: several blue plumbing pipes converged, each with a short section attached at a ninety-degree angle, pointing upward so the water fountained a yard or so into the air. Nearby, two big orange trucks were parked—the huge mobile generators powering the pumps. Behind the mega-generators, the lower path—where Biw had parked his motor scooter ten days earlier—disappeared into lush forest, deeply shadowed in the midday sun. The dirt road steepened for fifty yards and there it was: the hub of an international search operation and a media frenzy.

Canopies were arranged on and around what had once been a square of grass in front of the parks office. Now everything floated on a sea of caramel-colored mud, half a foot deep in places. Hundreds of people milled about, and all wore gumboots.

I walked counterclockwise around the square to get my bearings. On the right was the start of the upper path that led to Tham Luang. This area was taped off, aside from one access point through which rescue workers carried equipment in and out. The cave entrance was tantalizingly close, but just out of sight, blocked by trees. In the first days of the rescue, it had been a free-for-all, but now this was as close as the media could get.

Farther along were several large tents, shading equipment, and military-looking men. There was a storage area for scuba tanks—hundreds of them, lined up in silver rows. An air compressor rumbled, and there were regular loud hisses as the tanks were filled and sealed off. There was a whiteboard, surrounded by mounds of gear. The SEALs had their spot right next to the tanks. Next to them was the Chinese team, then the American military, then the Australians and the Euro team.

Farther up the dirt road was a gate guarded by soldiers. The area beyond this gate was off limits to the media; the buildings up there were reserved for the top brass. The path turned left at the gate, where a row of ambulances sat waiting.

Near the ambulances was a small building, which looked like the park rangers' office. I didn't know it then, but this was the war room, the setting of many crucial behind-the-scenes moments. Soldiers and police stood watch out front as journalists hung around, sheepishly trying to catch an eye and snag an interview with anyone who would talk.

From there, the path turned left again down the hill. Here it looked more like a scene from a music festival. Food, water, coffee, and personal items were being handed out by volunteers. It was an astonishing array of useful stuff, and everything was free. The volunteers, in their yellow shirts and blue caps, gave a surprisingly cheerful atmosphere to what was a grimly serious search.

Off to the right stood a bluestone toilet block that usually saw only a handful of people a day, but now had thousands using it. Sanitation workers did the unglamorous work of keeping it running, and volunteers swept out the mud brought in from everyone's boots.

Nearby was the medical tent and a rest area for families. A sign requested: NO INTERVIEWS.

I'd looped back to the start. The inner block was a square of mud we would come to know well in the coming days. It was where the authorities had set up a large white canopy for the media. Tables and plastic chairs sank into the mud. Reporters, camera operators, producers, and translators sat and stood in the makeshift press center. In the coming days, a second canopy would be added as the press corps grew.

We set up our camera, connected to Sydney using our LiveU (a device the size of a box of tissue that bundles multiple SIM cards to produce a broadcast signal), and did a live remote. Several mobile cell towers had been parked nearby to provide phone coverage and Wi-Fi. In between TV remotes and news gathering, I filed a radio voicer:

For Thai and Australian divers, today's main mission is to get to a T-junction in the cave, then go left towards a ledge nicknamed Pattaya Beach. That's where it's hoped the twelve young footballers and their coach are sheltering. But after more than a week of heavy rain, that part of the tunnel is now blocked by mud, which must be dug out. This is the biggest rescue operation in Thai his-

tory. International experts and Thai volunteers are flocking to the
scene to help, while the nation is on edge hoping for good news.

Jum got our official press passes. Mine was number 716. (At that stage, the Thai and international media were being counted together. Later, the Ministry of Foreign Affairs would work out that 631 members of the foreign media had registered, from 193 different agencies.) Jum then started working out the flows of information. The main source was the twice-daily press conferences given by Governor Narongsak, where he was usually joined by soldiers, who also spoke. There were also official groups set up on the Line chat app, but the quality of that information varied. Beyond that, we tried to catch a word here and there with the rescue workers—any new snippet to keep feeding the demand for fresh updates.

We scrounged two plastic chairs—not to sit on, but to keep our bags up out of the mud. Plastic chairs were a precious commodity. We worked into the night, establishing our presence on the ground, doing live remotes, and catching up on the story.

By Monday, July 2, the mood among the parents was understandably grim. They sat in groups at a simple resort near the cave. Since the boys went missing, Titan's dad, Tote, had held on to a sense of hope, and shared that hope with his wife and others. But today he couldn't summon any hope. Ten days. It was too long. He began to feel that maybe his son wouldn't be found. At least, not alive.

He started to cry.

The staff at the resort tried to cheer him up. A soldier came over and told him about all the things being done to try to get to the boys. It wasn't much use. All of the parents were miserable and exhausted and stuck in a gut-wrenching place somewhere between doubt and grief.

It wasn't just the parents beginning to have doubts.

Among the volunteer cave divers who'd flown in from around Thailand, there were some sobering conversations. A doctor friend shared with Pae a graph showing the chances of survival without food. By day ten, the chance of a child surviving was down to 10 percent.

"We were talking about, 'Okay, if [by] day ten we still cannot reach the boys, then we might need to change our strategy.' Instead of a rescue operation, it would be a recovery," said Pae.

A rescue operation involved pushing the limits of safety—putting lives on the line for someone else's. But the retrieval of bodies would be a slower effort, performed with care so as not to lose any more lives in the process.

The foreign volunteers didn't share their dark thoughts with the SEALs or the parents. They remained right on the edge of hope. It still might be okay; the boys and the coach might still be alive. They'd give it another day. This was still a rescue effort. Just.

14

"BRILLIANT"

By Monday, July 2, the water levels inside the cave were finally under control. Overnight, it had rained and the gauges went up a few inches but then quickly started to go down again as the pumps did their job. The war against water had turned, and the front line was being pushed farther into the cave.

"We had a really good feeling [that] this is it, this is the day we're going to get all the way through to the boys," said Pae.

The location of the Wild Boars was still ultimately a guess. But the clues scattered along the way seemed solid enough proof that they had turned left at the T-junction. Everyone was hoping they would be just a bit farther along, somewhere near Pattaya Beach.

But what state would they be in? Would they even be alive?

Ben and Pae said there was an agreement among the Euro team that it should be SEALs who would do the final push and—hopefully—find the boys.

"It's not just the publicity," said Pae. "It's about communication as well. Because we know the boys are Thai, it's better if they can have the SEALs team, who can speak Thai, going there and meeting the boys first."

Ben confirmed this account. "The plan was never to surface, the plan was to get close and get the two Navy SEAL doctors [there]—I promised the Navy SEALs. I said, 'Listen, I'm not going to go inside, I'm here to assist you guys. Make sure your doctors are ready with all the medication and the dry bags with food.' Because I can't surface, say hi and bye, and leave again. They're kids. You know, are half of them dead? You can't just see them and leave for twelve hours."

Ben and Maksym went in on that Monday morning and began tying off new rope along the cave, installing red climbing rope beyond the T-junction.

"I pushed two hundred meters [about 650 feet] of line, all the way past the restriction," said Ben. "Then it started getting shallower and shallower. I'm getting to Pattaya Beach. Next minute—end of the line. Okay, good, we are very close. Tomorrow morning, we get the doctors along."

John Volanthen has a very different account of the day. He and Rick started off from the T-junction, following the red rope Ben had laid. They came to a stretch of cave passage that had a black strap running along the length of the wall, made from the sort of flat nylon material used by rock climbers. That black guideline was an established feature of Tham Luang—something that had been set up to help visitors manage their way through.

John said Ben's line had been tied off at the start of the black strap and left attached to a rice sack still half-filled with rope. He estimated the tie-off point was one hundred yards from the T-junction, so they were still approximately three hundred yards away from Pattaya Beach.

Then the British divers looked up.

"There were a number of small polystyrene surfboards in the roof . . . bodyboards. So what would happen is that you would dry cave all the way to this point and there's a lake here. You would lay on the surfboard and you would use the black tape to pull yourself across the water, so you'd stay [relatively] dry and wouldn't have to swim. . . . But because the cave was flooded and the surfboards were polystyrene, when I got there, they were stuck in the roof," said John. "We cut off the spare line and the bag, and I carried that line forward."

There was no need to lay line through the next twenty-yard section; they could pull themselves along the black nylon strap. It led into what seemed like a tight pocket, but when they felt around, it was actually just the pinch point at the side of a passage shaped like a flat diamond (<>). Because the line led to the corner on the left and there was limited visibility, it felt like a squeeze, but by moving slightly to the right, the divers were able to pass through with ease.

Rick and John continued on, jamming their fingers into the silt to crawl forward against the current. They each had a 650-foot bag of rope, as well as the rest of Ben's bag. After a long dive, tying the rope to rocks and stalactites, they reached a rocky shelf and came up for air. They checked their tanks. Cave divers use a "rule of thirds" for their air supply—a third to go in, a third to go out, and a third as reserve. To make their cylinders last longer, the two men shut off their regulators and breathed cave air any chance they could, saving every last breath. They also deliberately removed their masks to sniff the air.

"We weren't expecting to find children; we were expecting to find bodies," said John.

They had reached Pattaya Beach and exhausted their rope supplies. They were right on the edge of their one-third air-supply limit and should have turned back, but they made a calculated decision to push on, to try to lay the spool of thin polypropylene line that John had. They even decided to stop laying the line through any pockets—only the flooded sections—in order to go as far as humanly possible that day.

And here an important difference arose in the philosophies of Ben Reymenants—who says he promised the SEALs he would stop short of Pattaya Beach—and the British divers.

John pointed out that the rescuers still didn't really know where the soccer team might be stranded, if they were indeed alive. The team had been trapped for ten days without food, so time was running out. The idea of stopping just short of them was preposterous, according to John. The two divers pushed on with a sense of determination and dread.

"I was absolutely expecting to find bodies in the water floating toward me," said John. "I've found bodies in water before; it's not pleasant. I wasn't looking forward to it. I was genuinely expecting to just swim into a collection of bodies."

As they entered each new sump, they had little idea what was in store for them. Would it be a fifteen-foot puddle or a long, flooded chamber? Would it be blocked with rocks, stalactites, debris, or corpses? They were about to start using up their "return" third of bottled-air supply. If they were to use up half their total air, they'd be forced to turn back and hope the down current pushed them out fast enough to escape before their air ran out. Every minute they went forward increased the risk.

"We were properly out on a limb," said John.

The British divers got into the water and submerged. Navigation was difficult in the murky passages. They were looking for a feature they'd noted on the map where the main tunnel makes a ninety-degree turn left and then another ninety-degree turn right shortly afterward. But there were also short offshoots to the cave, and the divers surfaced several times in off-route air pockets, having to then retrace their steps and try to work out which way was forward. They used their experience to look for ripples in the silt or indications of the direction in which the sediment was flowing, in order to determine which way was upstream.

It was hard going. They slowly progressed about eleven hundred feet until they came to a room-size chamber. There was nothing visible on the steep, muddy bank. John took the spool farther on and swam to the next fully flooded section. Rick was about to go back and cut the line so they could save a few feet and tie on again for the next dive. He took off his mask and gave the air a sniff. He called to John.

"Take your mask off and smell," said Rick.

"I did," said John, "and I could smell what we both feared was decomposing bodies."

Just beyond Pattaya Beach, on the ledge of Nern Nom Sao, the youngest of the Wild Boars was fading. His tiny body was wasting away.

"I felt faint and lacked energy and I was hungry," said Titan. "When I was very hungry, I tried not to think about food because it would make me even hungrier . . . but I was thinking about fried rice and *nam prik ong* [a Northern-style dipping plate]."

Food fantasies played on their minds constantly. It had been about 245 hours since any of them had eaten anything. Their faces were gaunt, their cheekbones protruding.

"By July 2, almost everyone was weak," said Tee later.

Their decline was not just physical. As another day passed, their spirits were fading, too.

"By the tenth night, we were losing patience, hope, physical energy, and courage. We could not do anything to help. The only thing that I could do was pray," said Adul, the only Christian of the group.

"I prayed, 'Lord, I am only a boy, you are an almighty God. You are holy and you are powerful. Right now I can't do anything. May you protect us. Come help all thirteen of us.'"

It was almost another birthday, this time for team captain Dom. Tomorrow, he would turn fourteen. He rallied the boys together, saying he wanted a birthday present tomorrow. He wanted them to help him dig with renewed energy and break through the back wall. He wanted to find a way out of the cave.

His teammates said they would help.

As it turned out, Dom's birthday present came early.

At around 8 p.m., the boys and Coach Ek were up on the higher part of the muddy ledge near their pee hole, now rather fetid. Some were digging, others resting.

"At that moment, I heard people talking," said Adul.

Coach Ek asked everyone to keep quiet. They froze in the darkness, straining to hear. At first, the boys thought their minds were playing tricks on them. Some came to an even scarier conclusion: ghosts.

"Pee Ek asked Mix to go down first, because he had a torch

[flashlight] with him at the time," said Adul. "Pee Ek said to hurry and go down, that was the sound of humans, hurry before they leave. Mix was afraid to go, so I said I'll go. I took the torch from Mix and went down."

Adul took off down the slope toward the water as fast as his weak body would carry him. But as he got to the edge, where the bank became steep and slippery, his legs went out from under him and he slid into the water. Once he clambered back on the ledge, he saw it was true. It really was people. Two men in diving gear.

"It was a miracle moment," remembered Adul. "At first, I thought they were Thai, officials or something, but the fact is they weren't. After they come up from the water, I was surprised, they were British. I didn't know what to say to them, so I just said hello."

By this stage, the rest of the team had walked down to the water's edge. Rick counted them as they came down and saw they were all there. A flashlight scanned across each one, a roving spotlight on a muddy stage. John turned on a camera, given to him to film the T-junction for the SEALs and for proof of life/death. He wasn't even sure if it had audio. It recorded the now-famous exchange.

VARIOUS BOYS: Thank you. Thank you. Thank you.
JOHN: How many of you?
RICK: [*faintly*] They're all alive.
ADUL: Thirteen.
JOHN: Thirteen?
ADUL: Yes.
JOHN: Brilliant.

Most of the team couldn't follow the conversation in English, only Adul and Biw.

"Anyone who knows English, please translate," asked Coach Ek.

Biw started to relay what he could understand from Adul and the foreigners. Tee urged him to translate faster.

"I can't catch everything they say, be cool," Biw told Tee.

Coach Ek touched Adul's elbow, urging him to ask the question they most wanted answered.

ADUL: When will we go outside?

JOHN: Not today. Not today.

ADUL: Not today?

JOHN: It's two of us. You have to dive. We are coming. It's okay. Many people are coming. Many, many people. We are the first. Many people come.

BOY: What day?

JOHN: Tomorrow.

RICK: No, no, no. "What day is it?" they're asking.

JOHN: Monday. Monday. One week and Monday. You have been here ten days. Ten days. You are very strong, very strong. Let's get up [on the ledge]. Okay, get back. We come. We come.

The British divers stayed on another bank to the left of the passage, separated from the boys by a channel of water. It was a deliberate precaution. They had no idea what state of mind the boys and Coach Ek would be in. They feared the starving, desperate team might try to rush them and grab their diving gear to escape. But after a few minutes, they quickly realized that the boys and Coach Ek were calm and posed no threat.

BOY: We hungry.

JOHN: I know. I know. I understand. We come. Okay, we come.

The boys and their coach moved back from the water's edge to allow the British divers to clamber up. The audio becomes unclear as the camera submerges. There is the sound of bubbles, interspersed with distant snatches of Thai.

BOY: [*in Thai*] Tell them we are hungry.

BOY: [*in Thai*] They said they know.

JOHN: We come, we come.

BOY: [*in Thai*] We haven't eaten. We have to eat, eat, eat.

BOY: [*in Thai*] Already told them.

The audio again becomes hard to follow as the divers talk between themselves and the boys talk to each other in the background. Adul's voice cuts through the chatter, carefully pronouncing each word.

ADUL: I am very happy.

JOHN: We are happy, too.

ADUL: Thank you so much, thank you so much.

JOHN: Okay.

ADUL: So, where do you come from?

JOHN: England, the UK.

BOYS (IN UNISON): Whoa!

They seemed genuinely amazed that two men from so far away had popped up in their cave.

John and Rick spent about forty minutes with the Wild Boars on their ledge. John took his thin line to the very top and buried the spool in the mud. He realized the boys had chosen an excellent spot to seek sanctuary. It may only have been about eight feet wide at the bottom, but Nern Nom Sao widened as it inclined, eventually ending about sixty-five feet above the waterline.

"It must be the only aven [vertical shaft] where there's that much height, that's easily accessible," said John. "An absolute blinder."

John and Rick wanted to raise the kids' spirits, so they asked them to cheer for the camera—a cheer for Thailand, a cheer for America, a cheer for the United Kingdom, and on it went. The boys' physical condition was remarkably good. They were gaunt but uninjured and didn't appear sick, even managing a smile.

The divers gave them flashlights. They had no food to leave, for the simple reason that they couldn't carry it. They already had three thirty-three-pound cylinders and a big bag of rope to try to manage as they pulled themselves through the jagged passages. John and Rick had pushed themselves beyond their usual safety limits and toward the end of their own carefully calibrated risk thresholds just to get that far into Tham Luang.

The divers promised they would send the SEALs in with food as soon as possible and that they would also return. They said farewell and started back through the sump, this time being carried along by the current. The trip took several hours but was relatively uneventful.

When John and Rick emerged into Chamber 3, they passed on the good news. They briefed the Thai navy diver supervisor and handed over the camera. The British divers gathered their gear and started the walk out. But by that time, Wi-Fi had been installed through to that forward operating base. News of the boys being found alive reached the world before Rick and John even got to the cave entrance.

Outside the cave, two of the fathers, Sak and Boon, watched from afar as Governor Narongsak strode over to the command center, as he did most nights for a press conference. They didn't think much of it; it would likely just be the usual: another night of slow progress, water levels, hopes, and determination.

Then a huge cheer erupted. The fathers ran over to where the media was crowding around the governor. All of a sudden, they were being manhandled, passed from bear hug to bear hug.

They'd found the boys!

They were all alive!

Sak's face was wet with tears. A big Thai soldier grabbed him and wrapped him up, his face clenching away the emotion that found expression instead in heavy slaps on Sak's back. Sak was happy, but bewildered. It seemed the impossible had come true.

"It's a miracle," thought Sak.

He struggled to explain it. Ten days in there. No food. He decided it must be due to karma—the good deeds of the boys winning out in the end. He thought that the mystic monk Kruba Boonchum was probably to thank, too. He'd predicted they were alive and would be found soon. And, finally, he thought that the vengeful spirit of the Nang Non princess must have relented.

"I believe she let them come out," said Sak. "I think she felt she kept them too long and felt sorry for them."

When the good news reached the resort hosting the volunteer foreign divers, including Ben and Maksym, the fatigue of their big day underground vanished. The Ukrainians produced a bottle of vodka, and celebratory shots were poured. They all downed one.

"Stop, stop, stop!" Ben raised his voice. "We might need to go back into the cave and help."

The bottle disappeared, and the team headed back to the mountain.

"I was still in my wet suit and immediately returned to site, where I found what I can only describe as a rave party full of cheering and crying people," Ben would later tell the *Phuket News*.

They'd done it—they'd found the missing soccer team. Now, they had to somehow get them out.

15
OPTIONS

With the boys and Coach Ek located, the priority was to get back to them with food and other supplies as soon as possible. The Thais took control. A team of four was chosen for the mission: a Thai army doctor named Lieutenant Colonel Dr. Pak Loharachun and three SEALs, whose full identities were never disclosed, which is common for special forces soldiers. The original idea was for two of the divers to stay with the boys in what was now being called Chamber 9 and two men to return with an update. They took a small amount of food with them.

The current was very strong, and it was hard going for the Thais, who were not trained cave divers. It should have taken around six hours to dive and walk to Chamber 9, and about five hours to get back out, helped slightly by the flow of the water. But that time passed with no sign of the Thai team. As each subsequent hour went by, concern mounted. What could be taking so long? Had one of the boys died overnight? Had a diver run into trouble? The rescuers waiting at Chamber 3 could only guess. The SEALs decided to send in three more divers to try to find out what was going on.

In fact, the journey in to reach the boys had been far more difficult than the Thai divers imagined. The water was cold, and the dive was long. They suffered from cramps and were forced to rest often. They eventually made it to Chamber 9 and met the boys and Coach Ek. But in getting there they had used up most of their air tanks. They changed the plan. Dr. Pak and three SEALs stayed behind with the boys, vowing to remain there as long as needed, even if that meant waiting half a year, until the rainy season ends—around October—and the cave drains—around December.

The other three SEALs took the remaining air tanks and dived back out. It was a slow trip. "Everyone was worried," said SEAL commander Rear Admiral Arpakorn. "They vanished for the whole night."

Finally, the three divers emerged at Chamber 3. They'd been gone twenty-three hours.

Deep inside the mountain, Dr. Pak and the SEALs got to work. The urgent need was to get some energy and nutrients into the boys' systems without overloading them. For ten days their small bodies had been in life-support mode, slowly breaking down the fat and muscle to supply a trickle of energy, enough to keep the heart pumping and the lungs expanding. At a chemical level, no food meant no glucose—the essential sugar that acts as an energy store for the body. As a result, their supplies of insulin—which regulates the blood sugar—dropped way down. In fact, many of the body's chemical processes had stopped, changed, or reversed. They were at risk of what doctors call refeeding syndrome, something first discovered in prisoners of war and now more often seen in anorexia patients. At this point of starvation, too much food could kill the Wild Boars. The rush of glucose would overload the body's by-now fragile systems. It would send their levels of phosphate, potassium, and magnesium into chaos. It would mess with their retention of fluids and sodium. The result could be delirium, seizures, respiratory failure, heart failure, coma, or even death. Although the boys were hungry and dreamed of huge plates of rich pork dishes and fast food, they had to be patient. The SEALs and Dr. Pak had brought in little squeeze packets of high-energy gels, the sort used by triathletes and long-distance runners. For now, these tiny shots of life would have to suffice, gradually bringing their bodies back from the brink.

For boys used to the tropical heat of Thailand, the temperature of twenty-three degrees Celsius (seventy-three degrees Fahrenheit) inside the cave felt cold. After so many days, they felt the chill reach into their bones. When they managed to smile, their teeth looked oversize in their gaunt faces. Dr. Pak examined each of the Wild Boars. Amazingly, there were no serious injuries. He placed all thirteen in the green category of emergency-response triage, meaning they needed medical care but not urgently.

Dr. Pak applied some antiseptic solution to the boys' scratches. "This will kill the infection first," he told one boy, as he swabbed his foot. "Then once you are out, we will find you a beautiful nurse."

The joy of finding the team alive was felt around the world. This was now the biggest news story on the planet. It had echoes of the Chilean mining rescue in 2010, when thirty-three men were trapped deep underground for sixty-nine days before being winched out, one by one, all alive. There is something about people being trapped underground that makes for an irresistible story.

Many countries have had a similar incident that has garnered huge media interest. There was the case of eighteen-month-old baby Jessica McClure, who fell into an eight-inch-wide well in Texas in 1987. Rescuers were relieved when they heard her singing a Winnie-the-Pooh song and managed to dig a parallel shaft to safely extricate her after fifty-six hours.

For Australians, it would be the case of Stuart Diver, who was trapped in the rubble of a ski lodge after a landslide in the popular resort town of Thredbo in New South Wales. He survived sixty-five hours in subzero temperatures, but his wife and every other person in the lodge was killed. Australians would also remember Tasmania's Beaconsfield gold mine rescue in which two miners were found alive two weeks after the mine's collapse.

For Li Shuo and the audiences in China, it was hard to know where to start. Incidents of people falling into wells and mine shafts were disturbingly common.

But the fact that this time it was children trapped and the added element of the approaching rains made the story incredibly dramatic, a real-life thriller.

The footage of the boys huddled in the dark on the muddy ledge was replayed over and over, with millions of people sharing John Volanthen's feelings: "Brilliant." But for those responsible for getting the boys and Coach Ek out, the celebration didn't last long.

"Initially it's a huge sigh of relief," Major Charles Hodges told the ABC's *Four Corners*. "Okay, the boys were able to find a high enough ground, they've survived this long. . . . But then it was—it was scary, because we realized how far back they were in."

People had been rescued from caves before—even flooded caves. But never had such a difficult set of problems faced a rescue party: the ages of the children; their malnourished state; the long, flooded route out; the uncertainty of the weather. It all added up to a stomach-churning dilemma for those now beginning to coordinate the extraction.

In an ideal world, the pumping teams would be able to suck enough water out of the sumps for the Wild Boars to wade out the way they walked in. But this wasn't a viable option: some of the passages were sixteen feet deep, and more rain was coming. There was just too much water.

Drilling was also out. Although Suttisak's drill team might have been able to bore a hole into the side of the mountain, it would be far too small for even the smallest boy to squeeze through. It would only be a way of dropping in supplies—and even that was a long shot.

That left three other options for getting the Wild Boars out of the cave. But which was Plan A, and which B and C, depended greatly on whom you spoke to and when.

The cautious move, at least for the moment, was to wait. The boys and Coach Ek were alive, and they now had energy cells, medicine, and company. Yes, they were all emaciated, but, incredibly, none of them had any serious medical issues. Perhaps they could simply wait out the monsoon, camping out on that muddy bank for the next four to six months, until the rains stopped and the flooded passages slowly drained.

There was also the possibility of extracting them via a yet undiscovered shaft, which would likely have been the safest option. But this also wasn't a feasible alternative—at least, not yet. Though much hope had been placed in the bird's-nest collectors of Libong Island and all the others searching the top of the mountain, so far they had found only dead ends.

Probably the riskiest option was to try to dive them out. The Wild Boars could all swim to a certain extent, but none had ever scuba dived. And even for a competent recreational diver, the way out was treacherous. For a non-diver, it would be almost impossible.

All options were on the table, and all were bad.

With the boys found, Suttisak's drill team had packed up their rig, and the helicopter had lifted the pieces back down the mountain.

On Monday evening, they had drilled about fifty feet through the limestone, piercing the cheek of the princess-shaped mountain, when an urgent call came in: stop immediately. Suttisak didn't ask any more. From the caller's tone of voice, he knew there must be a good reason for the abrupt halt.

They silenced the drill machine and air pump. Some of them started walking back down the mountain, flashlights lighting the way in the dark. Halfway down, Suttisak's phone rang again. This time, there was a chance for an explanation.

"This must be bad news for you guys, but good news for everybody," said the caller. They had found the boys and their coach.

Suttisak couldn't care less that all their efforts had been in vain. "We were very happy," he said.

Local folklore tells of a vengeful spirit haunting the Mountain of the Sleeping Lady in Thailand's Mae Sai district. LIAM COCHRANE

Top row of the Wild Boars (L–R): Night (16), Nick (15), Note (14), Mix (13), Tern (14), Pong (13). Bottom row of the Wild Boars: Coach Ek (25), Tee (16), Adul (14), Titan (11), Mark (13), Biw (14), Dom (14). LILLIAN SUWANRUMPHA/AFP/GETTY IMAGES

The boys and Coach Ek left their bicycles at the entrance of Tham Luang when they went in for what they thought would be an hour or so of fun adventuring.

APICHAT WONGNGOEN

The soccer team entered the cave just days before the danger period began, as described in a warning sign outside Tham Luang.

LINH PHAM/ GETTY IMAGES

John Volanthen was one of the two British divers who led the rescue operation. He's wearing all his gear so nothing gets misplaced in between dives.
LINH PHAM/ GETTY IMAGES

Bird's-nest collectors from the southern island of Libong joined the search, rappelling down shafts in the mountain, hoping to find an alternative way into the cave system.
RUNGROJ YONGRIT/ EPA/AAP

Pae (Ruengrit Changkwanyuen) gets a briefing from the military before he begins helping the Thai Navy SEALs with specialist cave-diving skills.
PICHAMON CHANGKWANYUEN

Australian Federal Police diver Senior Constable Justin Bateman, following the guideline into a flooded section of the cave. AUSTRALIAN FEDERAL POLICE

LEFT Members of the Australian Federal Police Special Response Group walk toward the entrance of the cave. AUSTRALIAN FEDERAL POLICE

RIGHT The author reporting outside Tham Luang during the search. The heavy rain caused the entire staging area to become a sea of mud. SUPATTRA VIMONSUKNOPPARAT

ABOVE Thai authorities and volunteers tried to pump the water from the cave, but the heavy monsoon rains soon flooded the entrance. NEWSCOM/ALAMY STOCK PHOTO

BELOW LEFT "Brilliant!" The moment the Wild Boars were found after ten days without food. THAM LUANG RESCUE OPERATION CENTRE/AAP

BELOW RIGHT This photo became emblematic of the international cooperation and strength in unity demonstrated throughout the rescue effort. THAI NAVY SEALS FACEBOOK PAGE/AAP

Parents of the boys kept a vigil throughout the ordeal, praying for the safe return of their sons.

LILLIAN SUWANRUMPHA/ AFP/GETTY IMAGES

Thousands of volunteers arrived at Tham Luang to cook food and assist with the logistics of the rescue effort, producing 20,000 meals a day.

ABC/BRANT CUMMING

Soldiers and volunteers worked to the point of exhaustion, sometimes sleeping inside the cave in between shifts.

KAMOL KUNNGAMKWAMDEE

ABOVE British diver Rick Stanton (right) and John Volanthen (in glasses) rehearse the rescue with volunteer children at a local school swimming pool. THAI NAVY SEALS FACEBOOK PAGE

BELOW The rescue in progress: a heavily sedated boy is carried through the cave by an international team of divers and rescue workers. SAKCHAI LALIT/AAP

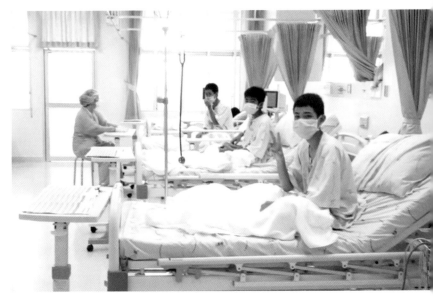

The thirteen Wild Boars spent more than a week (ten days) in a special quarantine ward at a Chiang Rai hospital as they recovered from the ordeal.
THAILAND GOVERNMENT SPOKESMAN BUREAU/AAP

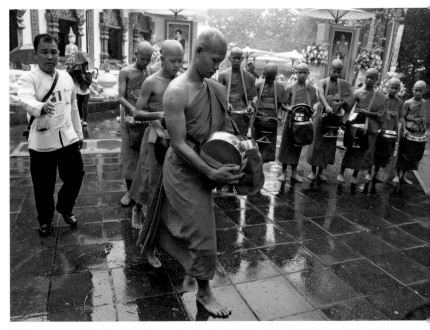

The boys were ordained as novice monks to show their gratitude for the sacrifice of others.
SAKCHAI LALIT/AAP

It was late, but he managed to book a flight back to Bangkok that night. Despite the sudden end to his operation, he felt satisfied. The drill team had overcome serious technical and logistical challenges to get that hole started. He was a tiny bit relieved too. He had felt the pressure keenly, and every night, his few hours of sleep were made restless with doubts and fresh plans.

"Job done," he thought, as he headed for the airport.

Suttisak had been back in Bangkok just a day when he received another important call. It was from a senior figure involved in coordinating the rescue.

"This is secret," the caller warned. "They [the divers] said the oxygen level in the cave is less than 15 percent; the kids can stay for only two days."

If the oxygen level dropped to 12 percent, it would start to become life-threatening. "Please come back to Tham Luang," the caller asked.

All of a sudden, the long-shot idea of piercing a hole through the side of the mountain to pump air into the cave complex wasn't sounding so crazy after all. Suttisak immediately booked a flight back to Chiang Rai. Then he called some friends in the oil and gas industry.

A new idea was brewing.

On Wednesday, July 4, the bird's-nest collectors were also summoned back to Tham Luang.

They were at Chiang Rai Airport, ready for their second-ever trip in an airplane—this time, back home to Libong Island. Despite their valiant efforts, they hadn't been able to locate any shafts that reached down to the cave complex below. They thought they were close once, having climbed sixteen hundred feet down a shaft, but that, too, came to a dead end. With the soccer team found, they were headed home.

They'd checked in already and were due to fly in twenty minutes when the island chief, Chaiyapruk Werawong, received a phone call. It was from the cave site.

"The soldier told us not to go back yet," said Chaiyapruk. "What we learned is that the army said taking the boys out is much harder than just finding them."

The wiry climbers grabbed their bags and ropes, and drove back to the cave. It seemed their work was not over yet, either.

Now that the Wild Boars had been found, there was a buzz around the staging area. Rescue workers moved around with a heightened sense of purpose. Reporters and crews worked all hours, repeating the little that we knew to the growing audiences. This incredible tale of survival against the odds, and now the question of how to get them out of the cave, was gripping Australia and the rest of the world. The ABC decided to send reinforcements so that we could cover the story around the clock. Reporter Anne Barker and cameraman Billy Cooper flew in that Wednesday, and were joined by freelance producer Boontin "Tin" Posayanukul. Anne would later work with cameraman Brant Cumming and Thai producer Angel (Achimawan Puranasamriddhi.)

With this team taking over morning reporting duties, David, Jum, and I went on a resupply mission. The bosses wanted to be ready to go live twenty-four hours a day, if necessary. We needed independent power, protection from the rain, and a space to work in the mud. We bought a generator, fuel, two fold-up tables, eight plastic chairs, a beach umbrella, a big waterproof tub, and a shovel. We were given a spot in the tent that we could work from. And later, when the morning team returned with wooden pallets—to create a simple floor above the mud—and a second beach umbrella, we set up a nice live spot, on an elevated muddy slope, with a view of the path leading to the cave and the air-tank storage area. The generator was out of sight at the end of a long extension cord.

We were quite proud of our work. Now we could broadcast no matter what happened. Plus, it was far more convenient to leave the tripod in place and simply step in, connect our LiveU to Sydney, and go live as the requests for updates increased. The level of intense interest, combined with the SIM-based technology offering a cheap connection, led to a workload that would have been unthinkable a decade ago, when a fifteen-minute satellite booking cost upward of $1,000. The flip side was that it left little chance to go out and find stories, with twenty or more TV live remotes booked some days, not to mention radio, online, and social media. Back in Sydney, Jonathan Flynn and other producers compiled footage and drafted scripts for our nightly TV news packages.

It rained on and off, and a rivulet soon formed. Our live spot was right in its path. As we stood around, waiting for the next live remote, David noticed something in the mud. Small green half spheres. On closer inspection, he realized they were the cut limes that were being used as a natural deodorizer in the urinals up the hill. The water was flowing down from the toilet block and running directly between the legs of our tripod.

During a trip to that stone-walled toilet block, I was surprised to see not one but two cameramen filming *inside* the men's room. There was an old Thai man sweeping the muddy floors with a long straw broom, and I guess they were filming a story about volunteers. It was a sign of just how desperate the media was for new angles, after days of coverage.

The media weren't the only ones trying to exhaust every possible option. While most of Suttisak's focus had been on the Sleeping Lady's cheek, there was another, little-known plan under way to drill down around where her feet might be imagined on the mountain, hoping to connect with the southern part of the Tham Luang system, the end of the six-mile-long cave. The geologists had scanned the earth below and located a large cavern of water that they thought they could drain and explore for a connecting passageway. The plan was to enlarge the hole enough for some of the American Special Operations team to venture down and try to reach the Wild Boars from the opposite direction, at the end of the cave. It was a long shot, but they had nothing to lose by trying.

Like Suttisak's other drill project, the southern plan had its challenges.

The drill spot was located in a narrow V-shaped valley, too tight for a big helicopter to get into. That meant that the drilling machine would have to be carried in by people. But the air pump was far too heavy to be manhandled through the forest. The closest they could get to it by road was one mile from the drill site. So that's where it sat.

The solution? Lengths of sixteen-foot-long gray piping were connected up all the way from the drill site to the air pump.

That Wednesday, when the pipes were connected and the percussive drill started its pulsing probe, rock particles were blown the one mile back to the air pump. Along the way, the high speed at which the particles made contact with the insides of the pipe generated so much friction and heat that the dust blasted out the end in a dangerous shower. The drillers had to regularly stop to avoid the system overheating.

When they finally reached the cavern, about sixty-five feet down, they were surprised. What had shown up on the scans as a dark-blue pocket was not in fact a cavern filled with water, but one full of sand. They'd been hoodwinked by the mysterious mountain once again.

16
POLITICS

In an operation of this magnitude, it was inevitable that politics would play a role. But whereas these power plays and negotiations typically remained behind closed doors, they abruptly came into the public eye with a shock announcement on Tuesday, July 3.

After delivering the good news of the team's discovery the previous night, Governor Narongsak was being feted as a hero. He had very much become the public face of this rescue operation, having been present at the site when the search began and leading the press conferences that were being broadcast around the world.

Governor Narongsak had shown up that first night in the clothes of a politician, a white shirt tucked into trousers. But in the days and weeks to come, his added yellow volunteers' neckerchief gave the slightly pudgy, bespectacled Governor Narongsak the look of a kindly scoutmaster. For more formal moments, he wore the military-style beige uniform of a Thai government official.

When briefing the media, he didn't waste words; he was clear about what he wouldn't discuss and often explained why. He took questions patiently, even if they were the same questions he had heard each of the days prior. He didn't snap or lose his temper, like Thailand's prime minister so often did when he addressed reporters. With degrees in geology and engineering, he was well qualified to command the various aspects of the operation, which he did so calmly and firmly. There was a sense among the public that Governor Narongsak Osottanakorn was the right man for this unprecedented job.

But suddenly, that Tuesday, the press was told to stop referring to him as the governor of Chiang Rai; he was being transferred to the smaller province of Phayao.

Transferred? In the middle of the rescue? What happened?

The story behind this transfer said much about Thailand. In fact, it had nothing to do with his performance during the search-and-rescue mission, and everything to do with power and money under the military junta.

Narongsak Osottanakorn had been governor of Chiang Rai Province for only a year. He had been promoted from his role at the Lands Department, where his reputation for integrity was impressive. As governor, he had ordered investigations into public projects that he suspected involved corruption, including a 300-million-baht ($9 million) water-processing facility and a 13-million-baht ($400,000) aquarium.

He knocked back lucrative projects that he believed served little purpose for the community and risked being used to siphon off taxpayer money into the usual pockets. This included a 50-million-baht ($1.5 million) tourism landmark and a 32-million-baht ($970,000) plan to build a statue of an ancient king in the middle of the Kok River in Chiang Rai.

The statue scheme in particular resonated with Thais. They knew of the problems surrounding a similar project in the royal resort town of Hua Hin, in an area known as Rajabhakti Park. There, forty-six-foot-tall bronze statues of past kings were built on army-owned land, overseen by the deputy prime minister. The total budget of around $26 million came from both public funds and donations.

But there were allegations of skimming. One palm tree cost nearly $8,000. For months, the government was adamant: no corruption here. A later inquiry into the Rajabhakti Park scandal found "irregularities," but nothing was done about it. There was no point in arguing: criticism of anything even remotely related to royal affairs came with the risk of fifteen years' jail time.

Governor Narongsak wanted nothing to do with that sort of bloated project. He wanted infrastructure the people of Chiang Rai actually needed.

"I'm willing to go anywhere, but I will not sign wrongful projects," Narongsak told the media in March 2018. "I'm willing to move to anywhere—as long as I won't have to deal with a mess like this."

The following month, that's exactly what happened.

His transfer order was signed on April 24. It was widely seen as a demotion. But the order wouldn't come into effect until July 7, right in the middle of the rescue.

It was awkward timing for the junta. The coup makers—led by the current prime minister, Prayut Chan-o-cha—had kicked out the elected government in 2014, promising to be tough on corruption. Instead, they had found themselves mired in scandals. Now, one of the heroes of the rescue was being booted for standing up against projects tainted with fraud.

The decision was explained only in the most superficial way. Minister of Interior General Anupong hinted at a juicy back-story, saying that Narongsak had problems working with other governmental units, but he didn't elaborate. There was no backing down from the junta. The order had been signed and published in the *Royal Gazette*, meaning it had been endorsed by the king. The transfer was happening.

Narongsak didn't address the controversy directly, keeping his focus on the rescue mission. Even though he wouldn't be the governor of Chiang Rai, he would continue with his role in the rescue.

"Let me confirm that the command structure here is still the same," he said at a press briefing outside the cave that Tuesday. "I'm still the top supervisor, as usual."

In the hours immediately after the Wild Boars were found, tensions between Ben and the British divers reached a boiling point.

Inside a neat blue canopy, with a string of LED bulbs overhead and mud below, the divers were briefing some senior Thai figures in the rescue. SEALs boss Rear Admiral Arpakorn was there.

John was tired after a long and physically demanding day of diving in the cave and had limited patience for what he called "gabbling" coming from the Belgian diver.

"Ben, either sit down and talk slower, or leave" is what John remembers saying.

Ben's version is that he was suggesting to the group that they start an immediate rescue attempt with a collapsible stretcher he had brought. He remembers John saying, "You don't make any sense at all. Can you shut up and leave?"

Others who witnessed the exchange have been reluctant to discuss the tension between the two camps. Vern blamed Ben's attitude for creating the antagonism, noting that other divers didn't have any problems with John and Rick.

There was another issue, though, and that involved the media. Among the divers, attitudes to reporters differed. John and Rick gave no interviews during the operation. The SEALs were officially prohibited from speaking. Many of the volunteer divers were friendly but guarded, preferring not to say too much about the Thai-led rescue. But Ben was quoted and interviewed several times.

On Monday evening, he gave an interview to Belgium's biggest newspaper, *Het Laatste Nieuws* (*HLN*), which included this quote, translated by *The Guardian*:

> *It's a race against time, because on Sunday heavy rain showers are expected. But we remain positive. We expect that the first two football players will reach the exit today, in the best-case scenario. It remains a difficult course through a labyrinth of corridors, with lots of diving and climbing. But the process is along with the current, and the visibility underwater is already a lot better. Moreover, they do not have to swim a lot. They have an oxygen mask on them, and they will almost always be kept on hand by one of the divers. In the third corridor there is air for breathing, where they will also be checked by a doctor. Then there is another 1.5 kilometers [0.9 miles] of climbing.*

There were two problems with this. First, he had just given away the top-secret and still-in-development rescue blueprint. Second—and this is not his fault—some news organizations reduced the quote in a way that twisted its meaning: "We expect that the first two football players will reach the exit today."

The next day, a memo went out banning Ben from the mountain. A piece of paper was posted at the entrance to the site, saying, "This person is prohibited from entering," accompanied by three photos of Ben.

It was a bruising end to a well-intentioned trip. Vsevolod, Maksym, and Pae decided to leave with Ben. There was a fresh lot of Thai-based diving instructors heading up to relieve them, and there was no point letting personal differences get in the way of the rescue.

Thais love uniforms. A security guard will take great pride in his tassels and epaulettes. Students wear uniforms right through university, keeping careful track of who is senior and who is junior to them. Low-level civil servants dress in military-style garb that shows their tenuous link to the kingdom's center of power, that amorphous nexus of the palace, the military, and the government. Even modern Thai society is based on hierarchy, and it's important to be able to see who sits where in the pecking order.

There were many uniforms on the mountain: military, police, military police, local volunteer rescuers, and the yellow-shirted Thai volunteers. But there was a handful of people who wielded great power and wore no uniforms at all—just a yellow name tag with a red stripe. They were so powerful, most Thais were reluctant to even mention their existence. They were the hand-picked representatives of Thailand's new monarch, King Maha Vajiralongkorn.

There had been a gentle sense of the king's contribution at Tham Luang. The palace had donated LED bulbs and other equipment to aid the search. His representatives at the scene preferred a background role, asking, "What do you need?" and promptly making it happen. But on Wednesday, July 4, something shifted. King Vajiralongkorn made it clear he was very interested in the rescue.

"Instructions were given by the king that [the rescuers] must bring out the children as quickly as possible," said Deputy Prime Minister Prawit Wongsuwan.

This proclamation might not seem like much, but many would later mark this as another important turning point in the rescue effort. Like the arrival of General Anupong, this reflected a shift in the power dynamics going on behind the scenes. Now that the king had thrown his weight behind the rescue, there was no limit to the resources that could be devoted to it. The pressure to deliver increased manyfold.

But to understand the role of this king in the rescue, one must go back to his father, the revered King Bhumibol Adulyadej.

The people of Thailand loved King Bhumibol in a way that outsiders often found hard to understand. Many thought of him as their own father. He wrote jazz songs that remain popular today. He was credited with various inventions and sent royal cloud-seeding planes into the sky to bring the rains. He was considered a demigod.

When King Bhumibol died on October 13, 2016, the nation plunged into deep mourning. His passing came after years of serious illness and hospitalizations, but his loss was almost unthinkable for many Thais. Hundreds of thousands gathered around the Grand Palace, holding his portrait and weeping. A year of mourning began. Almost everyone wore black. There were no major concerts. Even the annual Water Festival was subdued. King Bhumibol's cremation ceremony twelve months later was an epic spectacle, with an elaborate catafalque crafted by the kingdom's finest artists to hold his casket one last time before the smoke drifted across the royal field of Sanam Luang, ending an era.

His successor was his son, then-sixty-four-year-old Crown Prince Maha Vajiralongkorn. The public was less familiar with their new king, who had completed military training in Australia, the United States, and the United Kingdom, and now spent most of his time in Germany. Since ascending the throne, King Vajiralongkorn had made some decisive moves, including intervening to end an unseemly dispute about who should be the next supreme patriarch, or top monk of Thailand, and taking direct control of the Crown Property Bureau, estimated to be worth upward of $30 billion.

The kingdom was watching and waiting to see what kind of monarch he would be. But there was little open talk about the new king. Thailand has the world's harshest laws against defaming the monarchy, often known by the French term *lèse-majesté*. Among Thais, it was usually called "112," the number of the law that forbids criticism of the king, queen, heir to the throne, or regent. This number was close to the phone number for a popular pizza delivery service, so it became shorthand for the much-feared law: "Careful or you'll get a pizza." But the punishment was no laughing matter—up to fifteen years in jail for each transgression, with a 96 percent conviction rate. (For this reason, a full discussion of the current king or royal affairs here is not possible; self-censorship is the only way for a journalist to remain in Thailand.)

King Bhumibol had asked his people not to overuse *lèse-majesté*, but, over many years, the reach of the law had slowly spread to encompass anything vaguely related to royalty. In 2015, a man was jailed for making a comment about the king's dog that was deemed to be sarcastic. In 2017, a student activist was convicted and sentenced to two years in prison for sharing a seemingly mild BBC profile of the new king.

Over the course of the search-and-rescue mission, King Vajiralongkorn remained in Germany, with his young son. But it was clear he was watching closely. When the instructions to extract the soccer team quickly were given, his subjects knew they must do everything humanly possible to pull off this rescue. It was a royal intervention and one of the first major public—if discreet—acts of Thailand's new king.

Suttisak was also about to step into the role of a politician.

His new idea involved what was known in the mining business as "directional drilling." This is a much more sophisticated technique that allows long-bore holes to be made, using a drill bit that can change direction underground. But in order for this idea to work, he needed the right equipment and expertise.

On Tuesday, he posted his idea on Facebook. A friend from the engineer's university days called to offer his help. That friend now worked at PTT, the Thai-owned oil company. Engineers from the Thailand office of the US company Chevron also got in touch.

On Wednesday, Suttisak flew back to Chiang Rai Province and called a meeting at a secret location, away from the media, in a building not far from the soccer field where the Wild Boars had played their friendly match twelve days earlier. But the venue wasn't the only secret. He had invited the engineers from PTT without telling them their business rivals from Chevron were also invited. It was a risky strategy, but quite deliberate.

"When you work with intelligent people like this, they have their own ego," Suttisak explained. "It's better for them to come together at the same time."

As they arrived at the meeting, each party was surprised to find their commercial competitors there as well. Suttisak called them around a table. Thirteen men sat in plastic chairs, while others stood behind them. The engineer got them up to speed, holding up diagrams and turning his laptop around for them to see. Then he made it personal.

"I told them, 'Now we put the lives of thirteen kids on the table. . . . Try your best.'"

Suttisak had no idea how this meeting would turn out. Usually, Thais were used to working more as subordinates of a higher authority, rarely daring to question up, while Americans were the opposite, used to having their say. Chevron was also a much bigger company than PTT. But on the other hand, Thailand was PTT's home turf. Would the Thai engineers feel insulted or intimidated by having the Americans at the table? There was no time to work it all out; no time for clever politics. Suttisak had simply got the best minds he could find around a table and thrown down the challenge. Recasting the scene as a gangster movie with a meeting of Mafia bosses, he later described his strategy as "empowering the wise guys." But would it work? Or would it end up in an ideological shoot-out?

At first, it was awkward. Then, cautiously, the two teams began to discuss. They focused on the problem, and as the technical talk gained momentum, the rivalries soon faded into the background.

"This was an amazing moment," said Suttisak.

Suttisak also had some fresh information to share. That morning, he and his team had done an experiment in Saitong Cave. They had placed sensitive measuring devices called "geo-phones" at intervals on the outside of the mountain, several hundred yards from the cave. The engineers walked past Thanet's groundwater pumping team into the darkness. Inside the cave, one of them swung a sledgehammer, making a solid strike against the rock. The engineers could then calculate how long it took the shockwaves to reach the various geo-phones and use that data to triangulate exactly where the sound had come from.

They were confident they could replicate this experiment in Tham Luang, providing an elusive part of the puzzle—the exact location of the chamber where the Wild Boars were stranded.

The engineers from Chevron and PTT talked it over. Could they perhaps drill another hole into the cave system and drain the water? And what were the risks? Finally, they came back to Suttisak. Their conclusions were both encouraging and horrifying.

The directional drilling plan would involve building a tower and base, much like an oil rig. The drill would be sent down into the earth, then gradually make a ninety-degree turn and travel underneath Tham Luang cave toward the Wild Boars. A high-tech gyroscopic device fitted to the tip could track exactly where the drill was and line it up with the target: one of the deepest sections of flooded tunnel. The water would then drain through the drilled hole, hopefully to the extent that the Wild Boars could wade out. It could be a slow process, though: there were ten to fifteen fully flooded sections of the cave—depending on the water level—and the drill would need to drain each one. But at this point, every fallback option was worth considering.

The engineers thought it would take between fifteen and thirty days to prepare. Upon hearing that time frame, Suttisak immediately dubbed this scheme "Plan C."

But the mixed team of oil and gas experts had more to say.

"The result of the risk assessment . . . was quite frightening," said Suttisak.

They explained that draining the water from the sump might create negative air pressure, sucking the oxygen out of the cave. The boys, Coach Ek, Dr. Pak, and the SEALs would be dry—but dead.

Even if they equipped the team with oxygen masks, the engineers couldn't predict how powerful the suction would be. Suttisak worried that the pressure might burst the boys' eardrums, or worse.

Far from being disheartened, the engineers doubled down. What might work was *two* drills. They proposed that a hole could be drilled into the roof of the cave system and air pumped in. Then a second drill could pierce the bottom of the sump and drain the water. It would be risky. It would be expensive. It would take time. And it would drain only one sump before needing to be repositioned. But it was an option, and their job had been to come up with alternatives.

The next day, a brand-new directional drilling platform was made available by a major Thai construction company. Other parts needed for the rig were located and put on standby, ready to send from Europe. Within twenty-four hours, the complex Plan C was ready to be put into action.

Suttisak felt excited: he now had a lot to take into the war-room briefing on Friday evening.

17
THE LITTLE THINGS

The rescue operation was now of an unprecedented scale, with millions of dollars' worth of resources poured into the effort. But it was in fact the little things that sometimes made the biggest difference and kept people going when times were tough.

The Wild Boars of course remained unaware of the machinations happening outside. Once Dr. Pak and the SEALs had joined them, the atmosphere in the cave changed completely. It wasn't just the gels and medical care that they provided; their company lifted the Wild Boars' spirits immeasurably. They were no longer alone.

The inhabitants of Nern Nom Sao told stories and played games. The most popular game was checkers. The SEALs showed the boys how to carve out an eight-by-eight checkerboard into the dry mud with their diving knives, and make pieces out of mud. The rules were simple enough: use your pieces to zigzag across the board to the back row to earn a king piece, capturing the enemy's pieces along the way. It was an apt game. The loser was the one who ran out of options, their final piece trapped.

Only one boy didn't take part: Titan. He was too afraid of losing. The rest played for hours, moving mud around in the lamplight. The champion soon became clear and one of the SEALs, known as Bai Toey, was crowned "King of the Cave." Not much is known about the three SEALs, who remain semi-anonymous for operational reasons. But glimpses of Bai Toey's humorous personality would later shine through, when the SEALs appeared at press conferences wearing sunglasses and a surgical mask. Bai Toey got a big laugh when he introduced himself as "the most handsome one in the cave." The boys were amused by his habit of wearing just his underpants, with a silver space blanket wrapped around his waist. After the long days of isolation, the camaraderie the military men brought to the cave was heartening for the Wild Boars.

"I felt that Pee Bai Toey was like a father to me, because he calls me 'son,'" said Mark.

"I felt great," said Pong. "They'd find something for us to do and we'd have fun. They liked to tell us stories."

"We ate, slept together," said Coach Ek. "We became quite attached—just like a member of the family."

It was the same for the SEALs and Dr. Pak.

"For those nine days, we had to share everything with each other," said the army doctor. "Whether it's food or making sure that the children are happy and safe. I have a son myself and [the three SEALs] all have children as well, they are a similar age as our sons. Staying together makes us feel like we are a family."

The Euro family was also growing. Coinciding with Ben and the other three leaving came an influx of fresh diving instructors—Ivan, Erik, Mikko, and Claus—who'd flown in from southern Thailand.

Ivan, a Danish diver, was tall and lean, with a crew cut graying at the sides. He'd been in Thailand for twelve years and was co-owner of Koh Tao Tec Divers. His partner in the business was Mikko Paasi, a Finn. Mikko had dark dreadlocks and a beard. Erik Brown, another Koh Tao instructor, hailed from Canada. Claus Rasmussen was a mate of Ben's from Phuket, a co-owner of Blue Label Diving. All were experienced technical divers, with loads of cave dives under their belts.

But the diving at Tham Luang was next-level stuff, an endurance test for body and nerves. Over the following few days, the new recruits to the Euro team would be assigned tasks that sent them deeper and deeper into the cave. These jobs needed to be done, sure, but John and Rick were also verifying the skills of these four divers, whom they'd only just met.

Erik, Ivan, Claus, and Mikko delivered tanks and cleaned up the route, using cable ties to bundle wires and pipes and reduce potential snags. They also reorganized the way the guideline ran through the cave. This may seem subtle but actually made a huge difference. During the early days, when the rope had been used by divers without much cave experience, they pulled strongly on the line and often yanked it from its anchor points. This created a slack and meant the rope would pull tight against corners, and lead divers along walls rather than guiding them down a clear part of the flooded tunnel. At times the line led them straight into obstacles that could have been avoided. The new Euro-Scandinavian-Canadian team did their best to neaten up the route.

Often they'd be underground and wet for more than twelve

hours at a time. Sustaining themselves during these long dives was yet another challenge. They could take some water and snacks in for themselves, but it was just more to carry. Ivan found out the hard way that a certain brand of muesli bar didn't have waterproof wrappers. The energy gels helped. Mostly they just went hungry.

But the Euro team had a secret weapon. They had Moo. Moo was a Thai guy who quickly worked out how everyone liked their coffee and what their favorite foods were. Ivan was vegetarian, so Moo found the nonmeat offerings cooked up by the volunteers. The Euro divers would emerge from their arduous efforts to find Moo with a spread of delicacies ready. It was an extremely welcome touch.

But Moo had an entrepreneurial side. The border town of Mae Sai was flush with cheap goods, and Moo was more than happy to do purchasing runs for his team. Strangely, everything seemed to cost 100 baht ($3)—except, of course, the commando knives that Moo had specially engraved as mementos of the rescue. These cost quite a bit more—and they sold like hotcakes.

The little things could make a big difference—for better and for worse.

One of the big jobs was to get the spare air tanks into the cave. Each cylinder weighed fifteen kilograms (about thirty-three pounds), but they were often strapped together to form a forty-five-kilogram (one hundred–pound) bundle. Much of the heavy lifting was done by the Australian Federal Police officers and the Americans. All told, they would haul an estimated twenty-two tons of equipment into the cave. But the spare tanks still needed to be dived through the sumps to their designated caches. Much of this work was done by the Euro team divers.

On Thursday, July 5, Ivan had been delivering tanks deep into Tham Luang, staging the spare air they needed to get safely to and from the Wild Boars. He'd strap three cylinders together and attach them to his harness, trailing the awkward bundle between his legs underwater as he pulled himself along the guide rope, with another three tanks attached to his body for his own breathing.

Ivan was done for the day and preparing for the walk out. By now the pumps had partly drained the first two sumps closest to the entrance. But there was still the sixteen-foot section of flooded tunnel between Chambers 3 and 2—the S-bend. While most of the divers' equipment could be left at the Chamber 3 camp, this annoying puddle meant they had to, at the very least, use a tank, mask, and a helmet to cross it. As Ivan readied himself to head out of the cave, there was a glitch in a procedure that was usually muscle memory: "I put my helmet on, but I forgot to lock it."

As soon as he descended, the helmet lifted off the top of his head. Moments later, as he was feeling his way through the sump, Ivan's bare head bumped into the rock overhead. He cursed into his regulator.

The helmet was purpose-made for diving, worth a bit of money and absolutely necessary for this rescue, which involved dozens of head bumps each dive.

"I went down there with a flashlight for ten minutes, but I couldn't find it; it was soup," he said.

Ivan trudged back to the cave entrance without his helmet.

That Thursday night, we left the cave site and started to walk down the hill—Jum, David, and me. The evening news package had run, the late-night live TV remotes had been done, and we'd filed some material for the morning—TV and radio. The rescue operation was in a period of intense behind-the-scenes planning, with little shared with the waiting media. But there was still heavy demand for content. The beast needed to be fed. The main updates still came from the twice-daily press conferences led by Governor Narongsak. Frustratingly, the Australian Federal Police refused to do interviews. Their six men were playing a fantastic role, helping to carry equipment into the cave. We'd see them back at our threadbare hotel in Mae Sai some evenings, standing around the front courtyard still in their wet suits, half stripped to the waist. But their bosses didn't make it easy for us to tell their story to the taxpayers who funded them.

On the Australian military side, Defence Warrant Officer Chris Moc managed to get authorization to give me an interview. He was based in Bangkok and we'd met once with the Australian ambassador to discuss the unique role Australia had played in providing horses for the cremation parade for King Bhumibol. It was the Thai-speaking Warrant Officer Moc who shared a bit of horse-racing trivia that unites Australia and Thailand: the legendary horse Phar Lap was named after the Thai word for lightning. Thankfully there wasn't much *pharlap* in the skies as we spoke outside the cave, and the rain stayed away.

The Americans were much better at public relations. Their main spokeswoman was Captain Jessica Tait, the one who was "spooked out" during her first trip into Tham Luang. A thirty-year-old communications specialist of Korean-American background, she embraced her role at Tham Luang with passion, giving interview after interview, patiently waiting for cameras to be ready, suffering through the same obvious questions and giving what sounded like enthusiastic answers each time. Her energy was remarkable.

Captain Tait's role was to talk to the media so her colleagues could get on with their work: helping the Thais to plan the rescue. The Americans were widely credited by rescue workers for their organizational skills and ability to bring key people into the rescue efforts. They bridged gaps, connected people to resources, and took a leadership role on behalf of the foreigners at Tham Luang. Because the Americans chose to engage the press, Jessica was able to get across the message that the Thais were in charge and the US contingent were there to support them.

When I interviewed her for the ABC, she spoke about the joy of finding the Wild Boars alive as if it were the very first time she'd been asked. She talked glowingly about the spirit of volunteerism, about how wonderful Thai people were, and about the challenges of getting the boys out. It was just before America's national day—the Fourth of July—and she said there was no place they'd rather be than helping Thailand in its time of need. The Thais loved her. The media loved her. I suggested to the Australians they could learn a thing or two.

As Jum, David, and I reached the bottom of the hill, where the lower path led up to the cave, there was a watery hub of activity. The two big orange generator trucks were parked opposite a police checkpoint. Industrial-size lights illuminated the area in an orange glow. At the center was the fountain of water coming from the pumps inside Tham Luang.

We stopped to wash the mud off our boots, tripod, and light stand in this blue-pipe fountain. Others did the same as they came off the mountain. It had become a welcome ritual. This nightly ablution signified the end of a day's work. But there was something more. The water spouting from those blue pipes was a direct link between us and the boys stuck in the cave. It connected us to these Wild Boars, whom we spent all day talking about but had never met. And there was a sense of relief that every gallon that flowed out was helping to increase their chances of survival.

As we continued on down the road, lugging our TV gear, we barely spoke. It was dark and quiet and peaceful.

18
CRUNCH TIME

By Thursday, July 5, it was becoming clear to the international rescuers that there was only one option for getting the Wild Boars out alive. The boys were rapidly running out of oxygen, and the next big rains were forecast to hit in a few days, most likely on Tuesday, July 10. Rescuers faced the prospect of once again being thwarted by raging torrents of water. The approaching rains posed the very real threat of another retreat back out of the cave. If the monsoon really kicked in, they might not get another opportunity. Waiting out the monsoon just wasn't going to work. Suttisak's drill teams would take far too long. The bird's-nest collectors and other climbers had still not found another shaft to access the cave. That left only the riskiest option of all: diving them out.

At the time, the rescue organizers hinted that the boys were learning how to dive, and that's what the parents were told. Some media reported that each boy would be tethered to an air hose, swimming out with one rescue diver in front and one behind.

It turned out these details were untrue. Those who'd battled for hours through the muddy obstacle course knew there was no way the boys or their coach could make it out on their maiden dives. The conditions in the cave would be challenging even for an experienced recreational diver. The only hope was to sedate the boys and Coach Ek so the expert cave divers could carry them out, wearing full-face masks.

They didn't need to worry too much about depth. Any deeper than thirty feet, and burst eardrums would pose a problem for the sedated boys, who wouldn't know to squeeze their nostrils and clear their ear cavities to adjust the pressure. Fortunately, the deepest part of the flooded cave was only around twenty feet deep, according to Erik Brown's dive computer.

Using traditional masks and mouthpieces was out of the question. Both could be easily knocked off the face by rocks or extreme currents. The dive instructors knew that if beginners panic, they sometimes try to scream, spitting out their regulator. It doesn't make sense, but neither does breathing underwater for the first time.

But full-face masks have silicone seals that run from the top of the forehead, down the jawline, and under the chin, totally enclosing the face and allowing the person to breathe with both mouth and nose—something far more natural for a non-diver. Even if the boys were to lose consciousness, they should still be able to breathe.

There are several types of full-face masks on the market, with different ways of pumping oxygen into the face area. One type has a demand valve that opens only when the diver breathes. But for this rescue, the rescuers would use a "positive pressure" system that pumped a surplus of air into the mask. It was hoped this would gently force the oxygen-rich mix into the unconscious child's mouth and nostrils, helping to keep his airway open.

The biggest issue was size.

Dozens of masks had been procured, but almost all were made for adults. They would be too big to fit the smaller boys. Full-face masks are generally used for highly technical diving—salvage operations, military operations, underwater documentaries where the divers need to speak. None of these activities are suitable for children.

The rescue divers said around forty full-face masks had been flown in from around Thailand and the world. In the end they found only four that would work. And even *then* there were doubts about how the masks would fit the smallest faces.

Titan was just eleven years old, but thirteen-year-old Mark was tinier. Getting the right fit was a matter of life and death. Once the boys were underwater, it would be almost impossible to check their masks until the next air bell.

The international team knew they had to try to convince General Anupong that this was the best course of action. And they knew they had to be ready to execute as soon as he gave the go-ahead.

Getting a plan like this to work was like assembling a machine with many delicate parts: should anything go wrong with any of those parts, lives would surely be lost.

Two of the most essential parts turned out to be Australian cave divers Craig Challen, a vet from Perth, Western Australia, and Dr. Richard Harris, an anesthetist from Adelaide, South Australia. They had traveled the world diving caves, sinkholes, and wrecks, sometimes as part of an eclectic group of Australian divers who called themselves the Wet Mules. The strange name came from the expression "enough money to burn a wet mule"—as in "That man's so loaded, he's got enough money to burn a wet mule." But it also referred to the fact that they spent a lot of their time stubbornly hauling heavy loads of diving gear around.

Members of the club were intrepid in their diving, but modest to the point of self-deprecating. The Wet Mules' motto was Lurching from Crisis to Crisis, and their mascot was a red bowling ball named Colin. The absurdity of carting around a heavy useless object made it the perfect mascot for these quirky hobbyists. Their website was full of matey put-downs and photos of Colin the bowling ball with them on trips, as well as photos and reports from some of their world-class diving exploits.

They were a select group of people, brought together by a difficult and highly risky sport. Cave diving is a pastime that requires absolute trust: failure to prepare properly beforehand or panic during a dive can be fatal. The serious depths provide no room for error and demand slow ascents to allow the body to readjust to surface pressures and avoid the bends. During a previous diving trip in Western Australia, Craig Challen spent six minutes plummeting over 650 feet to the bottom of the ocean, nine minutes looking at the wreck of the HMAS *Derwent*, and then seven hours and forty-five minutes coming back up. During one of those long decompression stops, a shark circled his group for about an hour.

The Wet Mules' elder statesman, John Dalla-Zuanna, is philosophical about his reasons for cave diving.

"I just feel at home in a sense," he told the ABC in August 2018 during an expedition to Tank Cave at Mount Gambier,

South Australia—considered one of the most spectacular and most dangerous underwater caves in Australia. "It's just gliding weightlessly through space. I just love being weightless and all I'm hearing is my breathing. I can sort of feel myself get in tune with the water. You've got no phones, you've got no pressure about what you do at work. . . . We've driven four to five hours in each direction to get to here, and all that stuff, that all goes away. We come here on a weekend and we come here for the sake of experiencing something like this."

Craig is more enigmatic about why anyone would put their lives at risk to go cave diving: "We do have a saying that if you need to ask that question, you wouldn't understand the answer."

In July 2018, having recently retired, Craig had time on his hands to dive, and Dr. Harry had managed some time away from his anesthetist work. They arranged to meet halfway between their hometowns, to dive the underwater aquifers beneath the arid Nullarbor Plain. But, as the day of their departure drew closer, the story of the lost soccer team in Thailand loomed on the horizon. Craig and Harry tracked the story in the media and spoke with their friends in the tight-knit cave-diving community about the medical risks involved in diving the Wild Boars out.

"We'd been in contact with the British in the days leading up to this, so we were broadly familiar with what was going on in the cave and, yeah, to be honest, [it was] not looking good at all," Craig told the ABC's *Four Corners* after the rescue, recalling how he was feeling at the time. "It's a long way in, most don't know how to swim [a common misconception at the time], let alone dive, so we're all wondering how this is going to possibly work, and, to be honest, the prospects are bleak."

John Volanthen recalled seeing Dr. Harry's initial response to the idea, a text message that said something like: "That's bonkers, absolutely no way." But the British divers knew of only two cave-diving anesthetists in the world—the other was a Frenchman. Dr. Harry had also established the first sump-rescue training course in Australasia, teaching emergency-service workers how to dive into the muck and save the day. All that made him the perfect candidate for performing the highly delicate task of putting the boys under sedation in preparation for the dive, while Craig would use his medical expertise to perform checks during the first stages of the dives out.

When the official request came to help—the day before they were due to leave for the Nullarbor—Dr. Harry and Craig put aside their holiday and quickly changed plans.

"I had forty-five minutes to get to the airport," remembered Craig. "So in that time I had to unpack everything that I had, reconfigure, and get the gear that I needed for this trip and go."

Getting them covered by the necessary legal framework was quite a feat. In the background, dedicated diplomats and bureaucrats worked hard to get the paperwork done. For Dr. Harry to be able to put his unique skill set to use, two things needed to happen: he had to be registered with the Thai Medical Board, and the Thai government had to grant both of them diplomatic immunity. Neither of these was easy to arrange in a hurry, but Harry and Craig boarded a plane anyway. When they landed, they were kept away from the cave, still waiting for the paperwork to come through. The two Australians were the only ones who would have diplomatic immunity, due to the high risk of what they were about to attempt and the very real possibility they might be blamed for the deaths of children.

On Friday, July 6, the immunity and license to practice were secured, and Craig and Harry arrived on-site at Tham Luang. As they walked through the tent city that had sprung up outside the cave, to the restricted area where the SEALs and foreign divers prepared, the Australians saw some familiar faces. They knew Claus Rasmussen from a Thai cave-diving trip the previous year. For ten days, Claus had acted as a support diver as Ben Reymenants, Craig, and Harry explored the depths of Song Hong (Thai for "Two Rooms"), a tree-lined sinkhole near the southern town of Trang. Ben had previously dived down to 580 feet, and the Australians were keen to push deeper if possible. One day, while at 430 feet, Ben's underwater scooter suffered a "catastrophic implosion"—the loudest underwater noise the men had ever heard. Ben was unhurt, but some of his gear was damaged. He had to sit out while Harry and Craig pushed on the next day, eventually reaching 643 feet, before beginning a six-hour ascent. It was the sort of holiday the Wet Mules loved.

Rick Stanton was another diver the Australians knew well, an old friend of the Wet Mules club. Harry, Craig, and Rick had dived together at two world-famous cave-diving sites—the photogenic Cocklebiddy Cave in Western Australia and the mysterious Pearse Resurgence in New Zealand.

Craig and Harry arrived with little fanfare and kept a low profile—no interviews. They met with Rick and John, who had themselves requested that representatives from the British embassy join them at Tham Luang; they were worried that if things went terribly wrong, they might not get out of the country.

The Thais had their own diplomatic challenges. While the world's attention was focused on a cave in the country's north, another news story broke. A boat full of Chinese tourists had capsized in sixteen-foot waves off Phuket. The death toll grew by the hour. There were 105 people on board, and more than 40 of the tourists drowned. Soon questions were being asked about the tour operator, about the decision to travel in such seas, and about the Thai government's response. Tourism from China was booming and, at a geopolitical level, Bangkok was balancing its long-standing friendship with America against the rising dragon of Beijing. Rescuer Li Shuo and his team from Peaceland Foundation were torn: they wanted to go help their countrymen, but their mission was already established at Tham Luang. They were working with the Australians, carrying in tanks and other equipment, getting ready for a rescue—whenever that might happen. They decided to stay, and got on with the tough work of hauling gear into the cave.

While the Chinese and all the other rescue workers and divers prepared for a possible rescue attempt inside the cave, hundreds of people were working on top of the mountain to reduce the water flowing in. On Thursday, July 5, there was a serious accident. Four rescue volunteers were driving to the cave site when, at around 7 p.m., the driver lost control of the car. Their SUV plunged off a cliff and into the vegetation below. Three of the passengers sustained only minor injuries, but one was critically injured. A light drizzle fell on the scene as paramedics climbed down to the battered car in the ravine. It took a while for them to be able to safely move the critically injured person to the hospital.

After the British divers found the Wild Boars on Monday, July 2, they were relegated to an advisory role, working with the Americans to help plan and assist a SEAL-led rescue mission. The initial idea involved hundreds of air tanks being staged throughout the cave and a push forward modeled on a mountain-climbing strategy, known as a "siege."

"On a mountain you've got ten people [who] support eight people going forward, who support six, who support four, who support two, who support one guy who gets to the summit," explained John Volanthen. "That was the way the SEALs seemed to want to work. . . . The logistics were mind-boggling to be honest, but they're an army, I guess that's what they do in a battle."

I asked John if he thought that plan was something the SEALs could pull off.

"It would be exceptionally difficult," he said.

When Dr. Pak and the three SEALs were stranded at Chamber 9 on Tuesday, the other three SEALs emerged to describe how treacherous the diving conditions were.

"The attitude in camp changed the next morning, dramatically," said John. "They basically said, 'It's too difficult, it can't be done, we're suspending diving operations.' . . . They were very clear that the job is too difficult, [that] our men got back, but barely."

This was hardly surprising. Diving instructor Erik Brown later explained to me that any country would struggle with such a specialized rescue. The only way to save the seventeen people trapped in the cave would be a coordinated effort by the world's best divers and some luck with the weather.

On Wednesday, John and Rick became concerned that no serious moves were being made to resupply the seventeen people now trapped in the cave. They went to the Americans and asked them for MREs to take in.

An MRE—a meal ready to eat—was American war food, a modern-day upgrade on the C rations from the Vietnam War era. They're about the size of a thick paperback novel, with a thick watertight packaging. Each one would typically contain a main dish that could be heated by adding water to the inner packaging to create a chemical reaction. There'd be snacks like biscuits and spreads, maybe some preserved fruit, powdered flavoring for drinks, instant coffee mix, creamer and sugar, a dessert, and packets for salt and chewing gum. A plastic spoon would be included to eat with. But the Wild Boys and their minders didn't need all that; they mostly just needed the high-calorie parts.

Rick and John went through the MREs, throwing away all the surplus items. They packed enough for a week's supply into four tubular bags and did what they could to neutralize the buoyancy. They also packed a water filter, shiny space blankets to help everyone stay warm, and an oxygen meter.

"We told the Thais what we were going to do," said John. "They didn't help, but they didn't stop us."

Diving with this "monumental amount of stuff" proved to be extremely difficult, even for the world's best. The food bags acted as an anchor and made the hours of diving much more strenuous. Halfway in, John considered ditching one of them, but persevered.

When the British divers finally reached Chamber 9 with the bags of supplies, they told Dr. Pak and the SEALs to ration the food. They had brought only enough MREs for everyone to have about a meal a day for a week. But their cavers' instinct told him to be cautious. Make the food last two weeks, they told the Thais. At any moment a big monsoonal downpour could reflood the cave and make diving impossible once again. As hungry as the boys were, they should take it slowly. It was the first solid food the boys had had since they entered the cave twelve days earlier.

"I liked the MREs," said Biw later. His favorite was macaroni with chicken.

John and Rick realized they might have to take on the rescue themselves.

They called in backup. The British Cave Rescue Council began to mobilize two more ace divers—Jason Mallinson and Chris Jewell—as well as Mike Clayton and Gary Mitchell, who would help support the UK team. Martin Ellis, who had produced the most up-to-date map of Tham Luang for his 2017 book, also joined them.

Jason and Chris arrived at the cave on Thursday evening, and on Friday dived all the way to Chamber 9 to deliver supplies and familiarize themselves with the route.

One of those searching the mountain for undiscovered shafts into the main cave was an American named Josh Morris. The forty-two-year-old had lived in Thailand for many years and ran a rock-climbing and corporate team-building business in Chiang Mai. He was also a caver and a friend of author Martin Ellis. Initially, Josh had resisted joining the rescue effort, instead sending two of his staff to help, thinking they'd be better suited. But then Martin Ellis forwarded on an email from Robert Harper, who was looking for some climbing equipment. "Hang on," thought Josh. "My guys are there with gear. Why aren't the cavers talking to each other?" He wondered if his fluent Thai and understanding of the often-subtle cultural nuances might be of some use.

It was a tough decision. He was supposed to be going on a family holiday to the United States the next day, with his wife—a champion Thai rock climber, Khaetthaleeya "Kat" Uppakham—and their five-year-old daughter. But the holiday could wait; the rescue couldn't. Josh sat his daughter down and talked to her about how much the boys in the cave must want to see their mommies and daddies. The five-year-old eventually agreed that her dad should go and that she would wait a bit longer to see her best friend in the States. Kat had seen a familiar face on the television news, one of the senior military men leading the rescue. General Buncha Duriyaphan was a family friend, and Kat had taken Josh to meet him when they had first started dating eighteen years earlier, wanting to see if the general thought this skinny American kid was a stand-up guy. Josh obviously passed the test.

On July 2, Josh Morris drove to Tham Luang. He registered with the Department of Disaster Prevention and Mitigation, but when his name was simply written down on a muddy scrap of paper he realized he would have to find his own place in the rescue effort. He hung around the restricted zone where the divers and rescue teams were based until he met Pae on the Euro team, who introduced him around. He went to see the US military nearby, and by luck the first person he spoke to was Major Charles Hodges, the commander of the American deployment. Major Hodges said Josh could join a mission that night to explore a sinkhole on the mountainside. They were just about to rappel down into a crevice when a text came through saying the Wild Boars had been found.

Josh knew that getting anything done in Thailand required a network, knowing the right people. He kept reaching out to different groups—the Australian Federal Police, Robert Harper, and Vern Unsworth. Vern told Josh he thought it was a waste of time searching for sinkholes in the mountain that could reach the main cave. But he said diverting the creeks was important. The less water getting into Tham Luang, the better.

So, on July 5, Josh met up with Thanet, the groundwater expert. They spent the day on dirt bikes, hiking and rappelling to see if the water diversions above Monk's Series were working. On any given day there were around 150 people working hard at replumbing the mountain—mostly soldiers, but also volunteer rescue workers and local villagers. By then many of the creeks had been diverted, but each day more were being discovered. One creek was located almost above the T-junction, a critical spot. The problem was, much of the available plastic pipe had already been used up. Thanet asked the locals if they had any ideas, and they did. Not far away was a bamboo forest. Off they marched, returning with giant lengths of four-inch-thick bamboo, which were rigged up with sandbags to drain the creek off in another direction. Diverting the water was making a difference, some thought just as much as the pumping going on below.

The following day, July 6, Thanet and Josh planned to check out a huge cave. Thanet said he could probably get access to a helicopter to make it easier to get close. While they were discussing the details of the helicopter trip, Josh felt a hand on his shoulder and heard a vaguely familiar voice. It was General Buncha Duriyaphan, the one who'd vetted him eighteen years ago. General Buncha was a bearlike man, with a silver crew cut and a beaming smile, which had been on show a few nights before when he spoke to the media about finding the boys. Josh swapped contacts with the general, and they made plans to catch up when all of this was over.

It was about then that Vern and John walked by.

"They looked kinda long in the face," remembered Josh later. "I said, 'Hey, what's going on?'"

John asked Thanet to turn off his GoPro camera and explained the situation in detail. The takeaway message was stark.

"If we don't dive, everybody dies. If we do dive, some of them might have a chance to live," said John.

"What does 'some' mean?" asked Josh.

"I can't tell you," replied John, but he does remember deliberately using the term "multiple child casualties" again and again in various conversations, to make sure people had a realistic idea of the risk involved in the dive operation.

The British divers and cavers realized that a perfect storm was brewing, even as the literal storm loomed in the weather forecasts. If it did indeed rain heavily in a few days, the cave would flood again.

"Once the water comes up, nobody's getting in the cave. It'll be too hard to dive," said John.

That was new information to Josh. He had figured—as most of us had—that if the divers could reach the boys now then they could continue to resupply them. But, in fact, if the cave flooded again, they might be cut off once again. The boys, Coach Ek, and the four SEALs had one hundred MREs—so even if they rationed their food to one meal a day, that was only enough for another six days.

Then there was the oxygen level. As the Wild Boars and their minders breathed, they used up the oxygen and exhaled carbon dioxide. Eventually the balance would become dangerous. Inhaling too much carbon dioxide causes fatigue and confusion; soon the boys, their coach, and their would-be saviors would drift off to sleep and die.

Either way, the approaching rains were probably a death sentence.

Josh had just been in a meeting with two senior military figures, and they weren't talking with the same urgency as John and Vern. Josh wanted to at least make sure the decision makers were fully aware of the British divers' opinion, that they grasped the gravity of the situation.

Fortunately he had the Thai-language skills to get the message across, and he had an "in"—his wife's connection with General Buncha. The general met with Josh.

"We have to dive, sir," Josh told General Buncha, and relayed John's dire ultimatum. "If we don't, everybody will die. If we do dive, some might die. But if we don't dive, you're just going to collect seventeen bodies."

Even as they spoke, death was stalking Tham Luang. While the divers and soldiers tried to weigh up the risk–reward ratio of a rescue attempt, tragedy struck.

Saman Gunan was known to his friends as "Ja Sam," or Sergeant Sam. The thirty-seven-year-old had once been a member of the elite Thai Navy SEALs, but later took on a security role at Suvarnabhumi Airport in Bangkok.

There were some fit men helping with the search, but few could have competed with Saman. He'd won triathlons in Thailand, but it was when he made the switch to adventure sports that Saman really hit his stride. Fellow extreme athlete Ryan Blair remembered seeing the Thai for the first time as they competed in the River Kwai Trophy, a grueling run-swim-kayak-bike-run-bike-run-swim festival of pain that is Thailand's biggest adventure race.

"My teammate Piers and I were in the lead a couple of hours into the race and thought we had a comfortable cushion until this strong-looking biker comes up from behind with his team-mate and was smiling. We were melting and suffering under the Thai summer sun—how could this guy be smiling?!"

Ryan Blair was so impressed with Saman that he signed him up as a member of the North Face Adventure Team, a group of elite multisport athletes from across Asia. Saman had podium finishes in Malaysia and China, sometimes individually or as part of a team. When he trained shirtless under the hot Thai sun, scars were visible across his chest, the result of a mysterious blood disease in his younger days.

"He raced like there was no tomorrow and often past his limit. His enthusiasm was boundless, and his heart was stronger than his powerful legs," said Ryan. "He was the only person I knew who, after running fifty kilometers [thirty-one miles] or four-plus hours of adventure racing, would then do push-ups at the finish line, just to show us his power and, most important, make us smile."

One anecdote from his friend Ryan said a lot about Saman's character. He had traveled to Hong Kong to help friends in an ultra-endurance event. His job was to run with them for a twenty-five mile stretch, carrying their water bottles and food. But Saman got so caught up in the moment that he refused to stop at the crew car and kept on running until his legs gave out.

"By then it was dark and he was in the middle of Tai Mo Shan region . . . with no headlight, jacket, or map, and he had just arrived in Hong Kong for the first time and only spoke Thai! He went missing for hours, and our support crew wondered where he was and then he suddenly appeared smiling and told the story [of] how he found and followed a few different other teams . . . and ate from some checkpoints. It was such classic Saman," remembered Ryan.

The day Saman was deployed to Tham Luang—Sunday, July 1—he decided to make a quick selfie video while standing beneath the wing of the plane.

"We are ready to fly to Chiang Rai," he said, the sky a deep blue behind him and a reflected horizon line bisecting his wraparound sunglasses.

"For me, I came with the Suvarnabhumi Airport team under the Airports of Thailand Public Company, the sponsor for this event. In addition, an underwater medical team from the navy is joining us. Also, a team from Sea World Diving is with us and has sponsored a lot of equipment for us to use in this operation."

He looked relaxed, maybe even a bit excited to be joining his buddies for some commando-style work once again.

"Will be seeing you this evening at Tham Luang, Chiang Rai. May luck be with us in bringing those children home."

Since arriving at the cave site, Saman Gunan had leaped wholeheartedly into his role as a support diver. At around 10:30 a.m. on Thursday, July 5, he and his dive buddy were given an important mission—to each take three spare scuba tanks and leave them in one of the inner chambers, ready for any rescue effort.

It was hard work inside the flooded tunnels. The men had three tanks for themselves, plus the three spare tanks strapped together that they dragged between their legs. The water was cold, the passage often tangled with wires and pipes and obstructed by sudden outcrops of rock. It was an underwater obstacle course, with just a few inches' visibility. But Saman Gunan was in top shape.

He and his buddy had delivered their tanks—they completed their mission—and paused for a rest before the arduous trip back. They ate power bars and energy gels. Then they each strapped their three remaining tanks on and began their journey out.

What happened next is shrouded in mystery. Even SEAL commander Rear Admiral Arpakorn Yuukongkaew has only a vague idea of what happened to Sergeant Sam.

The buddy was right behind him, but it was dark. There was one part when Sam was diving and he just stopped still. We don't know why. The diving buddy followed him and saw that he was motionless, so the buddy touched him and still there was no reaction. So he touched his face and found out the mouthpiece had slipped from Sam's mouth. He then put the mouthpiece back for Sam and dived him out to where he could do first aid, CPR. He was unconscious and couldn't be revived.

Saman's dive buddy returned to Chamber 3 at 1:30 a.m. Friday morning, fifteen hours after he set off. What hell that man must have gone through as he fumbled back through the dark cold water alone can only be imagined. Other Thai divers headed in to retrieve Saman's body.

Later that day, Governor Narongsak announced the awful news. The optimism buzzing around the mountain was shattered. Activity slowed, and there was an audible quietening at the operations area.

The SEALs were determined to honor their colleague by getting the Wild Boars out.

"We will not stop our mission, we will not let the sacrifice of our friend go to waste," Rear Admiral Arpakorn told reporters at the scene.

So what happened? What caused this supremely fit man to suddenly die?

The first reports from officials were confusing.

"His job was to deliver oxygen. He did not have enough on his way back," Passakorn Boonyalak, Chiang Rai's deputy governor, told the media later.

But that was wrong, according to the SEAL commander.

"He had three tanks with him. Each tank had its own regulator, and none of the tanks was empty," said Rear Admiral Arpakorn. "It's not like in the news reports, that he only had one tank, no reserve. We had a lot of reserves."

"Exactly what happened, I don't think anybody knows," said Ivan, the expert technical diver from Koh Tao. "The list of things that could have happened is almost endless."

One of the least likely scenarios is that he simply ran out of air, said Ivan, echoing the SEAL commander's analysis. Not for an experienced diver, with three tanks strapped to his body and fresh tanks stationed throughout the cave. Ben Reymenants wondered if Saman had picked up a "foul tank," contaminated with fumes or perhaps too much carbon monoxide or carbon dioxide.

"Overexertion is much more likely; overexertion creating a massive amount of carbon dioxide that eventually will put your brain to sleep," speculated Ivan. "The conditions don't allow us to get the full picture."

This ambiguity is typical for diving deaths. Most doctors will list suffocation or water in the lungs as the cause of death on the death certificate, because that's what eventually kills the diver. But the question of what created the emergency often goes unanswered. In near-zero visibility, the mystery only deepens. Even Saman's dive buddy just yards away was oblivious as to why his friend suddenly stopped moving.

"Diving in the cave is always dangerous," said Rear Admiral Arpakorn. "The cave itself is complex, so if we aren't careful, there are lots of ways to die."

The same thought spread across the mountain, and then across the world. If a fit former SEAL could die, what chances did the Wild Boars have of getting out of the cave alive?

The death of Saman Gunan cast a pall over the rescue operation. But there was no time to mourn. There was still a job to be done.

Since Josh Morris had spoken with General Buncha, things had moved at lightning speed. Josh fell into a coordinating role, helping to communicate the views of the experts to the decision makers in a series of meetings that involved some of the most powerful people in the kingdom. Three separate sessions led to an emergency meeting being called in the war room that evening.

By dark, the pitched-roof building that housed the war room was surrounded by a restless throng of media. Expectations were growing. The boys and Coach Ek had now been in the cave for two weeks.

There were five items on the agenda that evening. The first was a briefing about the diving option. The last item was Suttisak, who was keen to share his new plan—the slow but precise directional drilling.

The war room had now been moved out from the side room to the main space inside the parks office, where it could accommodate more people. General Anupong Paochinda was there, along with top brass from the navy and army, police chief Commissioner-General Chakthip Chaijinda, senior government officials, the US military leaders, Gary Mitchell from the British Cave Rescue Council, Suttisak, Josh, and others. Everyone knew the stakes were high. The international team began to make their pitch, led by the US mission commander, Major Charles Hodges.

"I told him that, 'Sir, the eyes of the world are watching us,'" Major Hodges recounted for the ABC's *Four Corners*. "'We've got twelve kids and a soccer coach that are trapped here. We've got emotions at a, uh, a significant level here . . . and unfortunately, in these types of situations, emotions are not your friend. Emotions are not helping us to make sound decisions.'

"And I told the minister of the interior, 'Sir, we are looking at this only from a logical standpoint. We are trying to remove all emotion.' But now we're getting to the point where we only had one option, and if we didn't make the choice to dive, then the circumstances surrounding the situation would make the decision for us."

General Anupong listened carefully. He asked questions about their plan.

After about an hour, General Anupong rose from his seat, walked to the front of the room, and spoke quietly to those giving the briefing. Suttisak was sitting nearby, but he couldn't make out their conversation.

"After that the minister of interior kind of walked back to his chair, [but] before that he touched the shoulder of this guy, this guy, this guy . . . [and said] 'Let's go into the small room,'" he recalled.

The anointed ones included Police General Chakthip Chaijinda, Major Charles Hodges, Master Sergeant Derek Anderson, Gary Mitchell, Josh, and Thanet. They got up and followed the general into the small room.

With that, the meeting was over. Suttisak never got to speak a word. There was no formal announcement, but those in the room knew the decision had been made.

The international team would be diving the Wild Boars out.

The rescue was imminent.

OUT OF
THE CAVE

19
PREPARATIONS

In order to give their plan every chance of success, the rescuers prepared in every way they could think of.

The rehearsals started at a school six miles from the cave, in Mae Sai. It was Saturday, July 7, the morning after the dive option had been decided upon. At Pornpikul Wittaya School's indoor swimming pool, the colorful foam paddleboards had been packed away neatly. There would be no regular swimming lessons that day. The pool had been taken over by a select group of Thai Navy SEALs and US soldiers, as well as the British divers, for a secret practice run. In these controlled conditions, the team would simulate the most dangerous part of the operation: putting a child underwater and swimming him out.

Standing around the pool were three boys of small, medium, and tall builds—roughly the same sizes as the boys trapped in the cave. The boys had volunteered for the job. Paramedics looked on, first-aid kits open at the ready.

"There were a ton of medical people, and they were obviously very concerned we were going to drown these children," said John Volanthen.

The rescuers put each boy into a wet suit, put a buoyancy vest on them, and finally strapped an air tank to their fronts. To do this, the divers had modified a harness, adding a handle on the back to carry the boy and bungee straps to the front to attach the cylinder—known to cave divers as a "bottle bra." They added a lead weight to a pocket in the front. The theory was that if something went wrong and the boy somehow separated from his chaperone, the weight of the tank and lead would drag him to the bottom of the cave, still facedown. With luck, he would remain there—breathing—until the diver could find him again.

The first boy stepped into the water. John and Rick knelt around him and put on the full-face mask. Rick was behind the boy, pulling the straps tight, while John—still wearing his spectacles attached by a red neoprene strap—checked that the silicone seal was tight and the hoses were all functioning as they should.

Satisfied that the mask was on tightly, they carefully submerged the boy facedown, standing over him, watching through the clear water. Bubbles rose from the mask. It was working. Then a diver with side-mounted air tanks took control of the boy, swimming just below the surface, holding the boy underneath him. More bubbles surrounded them. Bubbles were a good sign. In fact, in the murky water inside the cave, the bubbles would be the only sign of life available to the rescue divers. The divers practiced passing the boys to each other, transitioning from water to land, and getting them in and out of their diving gear. The boys were told to try to stay still, like the soon-to-be-sedated Wild Boars.

John and Rick felt the mood change. Until now, all their diving had been deep inside a cave in murky water. Though it was clear the British men were able to dive in and out of the cave much better than anyone else, the Thais hadn't actually witnessed their skills and methodical approach. After about an hour, John looked up from the swimming pool to see the medics on their phones, no longer watching them like hawks, convinced that no kids would drown today.

"There was a change in the demeanor of the people watching us and there were phone calls made, and to me that was the moment when I think people started to realize that what we were saying was possible."

The practice run was a success. The team had shown they could put a young non-diver underwater using a full-face mask and a front-mounted tank, and move around. But this was in the relatively pristine environment of a school swimming pool. Would it work in the dark, flooded tunnels?

The divers had rehearsed their jobs; now it was time for the whole rescue team—the British divers, the Euro team, the SEALs, and the volunteers from Australia, the United States, China, and Thailand—to put the overall plan through its paces.

The Americans suggested an ROC drill—a rehearsal of concept. As Ivan later put it, "An ROC drill is what you see in the movies, commando movies, when they're sitting outside about to do this raid on the enemy and they take rocks and branches and say, 'Okay, this is the command post, this is you guys.' And they move it around to give a visual briefing of the mission."

In the dimming light of evening, the parking lot above the row of ambulances became a miniature Tham Luang, a scaled-down two-dimensional representation of the cave layout. The various actors in the rescue stood around, as if they were giants looking down through the mountain.

"We built the entire cave, with the tunnels, the chambers, to scale," remembered Ivan.

Instead of rocks and branches, the rescuers used sixteen-ounce plastic water bottles to represent the key assets, wrapped in color-coded tape.

"We had bottles with red tape—they were kids—so we had thirteen red bottles lying on a chair with a number nine on [it]," said Ivan, referring to Chamber 9, Nern Nom Sao.

"Then we had bottles with blue tape—they were normal air tanks," he said. These spare tanks were positioned at various stages of the tunnel. Once the rescue was under way, empty cylinders would be marked with a red glow stick that would last about twelve hours and be removed by support divers, where possible.

"We had green bottles—bottles with green tape—they in-dicated oxygen or Nitrox80 tanks that were to be used for the kids." These special tanks had a mix of 80 percent oxygen, rather than the usual 21 percent found in air. The reason was sobering. The divers wanted to deliberately flood the boys' system with oxygen so that if things went wrong, they would have extra time to perform a successful resuscitation. Essentially, the boys could be dead for longer and still brought back to life.

The top leaders of the Thai government and military walked over to observe. The rescuers formed into teams according to the roles they would play in the rescue. Dr. Harry would sedate the Wild Boars, and Craig would do the first medical checks in Chamber 8. Then there were the recovery divers, who would transport the boys: this job would be taken on by the British

specialists—Rick, John, Chris, and Jason. The support divers—
Craig, Ivan, Erik, Mikko, and Claus (others would soon join)—
would be waiting in some of the chambers to assist with getting
the boys out of their dive gear and carrying them to the next
sump. Once the "packages" reached Chamber 3, the boys would
be checked by US medics, put onto stretchers, and carried across
the slippery obstacle course to the entrance.

"We started role-playing," said Ivan.

The ROC drill quickly showed flaws in the plan.

"Stop, stop, stop, stop. Everybody back," shouted someone, at
the first stumble.

As the giants stepped through their plan, moving red, blue,
and green water bottles from chair to chair, it became clear that
some of the tanks needed to be repositioned. They noted down
the changes and started again.

"Stop, stop, stop, stop. That doesn't work."

Once they'd ironed out the biggest kinks, the overall plan
worked, but the divers realized they each had a slightly different
mental image of the cave layout. This wasn't surprising, given
the near-zero visibility underwater and the pitch black above
the water. They realized that a diver going blindly through the
brown soup, hand after hand on the guide rope, could simply
swim past an embankment or a cluster of tanks, conscious only
of a rock he brushed alongside or—more often—the sudden
donk as his helmet crashed into an unseen rock ahead.

Outside, in the bright tropical sunlight of the parking lot, the
divers stood around the chairs and taped-up water bottles and
lines in the dirt, and continued debating the layout of the cave.
Their navigational clues were specific, understandable only to
a handful of people in the world: "Yeah, you know when you

come up and you have that stalactite, yes, that's number 5, good, and number 6 is, you know, when you just come around that corner, where you have the double knot, yes, that's 6."

In some chambers the rope ran out of the water and up the bank, so the divers couldn't miss the stop. But the fuzziest location in their collective minds was Chamber 6—the long, tunnel-like chamber, flanked by muddy banks. The British divers had a preferred spot for the temporary de-gearing and checkup station within Chamber 6, but Ivan and Erik weren't 100 percent sure that's where the tanks had been left. Even a sliver of doubt was an unacceptable risk for these highly trained technical divers.

A simple solution was created.

Two large numbers—5 and 6—were printed in black ink onto pieces of white sheets of paper, which were then laminated. The following day, Rick and John would carry them in as they dived toward the boys, clipping the numbers on to the guideline exactly where they wanted the spare air tanks and the support divers to be waiting.

The ROC drill had a twofold practical purpose: to visualize the rescue and to dry-run everyone's roles. But like the swimming pool rehearsal, it was also a chance for the foreigners to demonstrate their capabilities.

"The drill was useful-ish," said John Volanthen. "But I think the key thing was, it demonstrated to the governor and whoever that there is actually a plan and it is organized and there is some chance of success."

The arrival of Dr. Harry, an anesthetist, might have suggested that perhaps some kind of sedation would be involved in the rescue. But at the time, this was a closely guarded secret.

In a testament to the old adage "never believe something until it's officially denied by the government," Thailand's prime minister, General Prayut Chan-o-cha, refuted claims that the boys would be unconscious.

"Who would chloroform them? If they're chloroformed, how could they come out? It's called an 'anxiolytic,' something to make them not excited, not stressed," he told the press in Bangkok on July 10, adding that the antianxiety pills were the same medication he took to relax before shooting guns. At this, he raised an imaginary rifle and pulled the imaginary trigger.

But in fact, a powerful sedative would be used to knock the boys out during the rescue. They would be completely unconscious; it was their only chance of getting out of the cave alive.

One of the biggest threats to the rescue operation was the possibility of the boys panicking underwater. As Craig Challen later told the ABC's *Four Corners*: "If you put me in a full-face mask with no previous experience and dragged me out of the cave—it's about a three-hour trip—then I would be terrified and probably panicking as well." Medically sedating the boys was considered the only way to save their lives.

For Dr. Harry, the question was: What cocktail of drugs should he use? What do you give malnourished boys so that they stay still, and aren't traumatized by being dragged underwater through a hostile cave environment? This kind of rescue had never been attempted before, so there was no rule book. Dr. Harry consulted widely, seeking the opinions of other medical experts in Thailand and abroad.

In the end, the anesthetist came up with a combination of three drugs. First, he would give them a 0.5 milligram oral dose of alprazolam, an antianxiety drug better known by its trade name Xanax. Giving the boys a tablet of this while they were still with their friends would hopefully take the edge off any fear they had as they prepared to leave.

Next, he would inject ketamine into a muscle in one of their legs; this would be the main sedative. A powerful drug originally developed as an animal tranquilizer, it was also used as a pain-killer for humans and, in more recent times, as a recreational drug by partygoers. It was known to knock out memories—perfect for the job inside Tham Luang.

Dr. Harry would use five milligrams of ketamine per kilogram of body weight, to put the boys to sleep. Ketamine acts fast but doesn't last long—about an hour. The rescue, however, would take several hours. This meant that Dr. Harry had to instruct each of the recovery divers how to readminister the drug using a syringe preloaded with a top-up dose of two and a half milligrams for every kilogram of body weight. The divers would carry the syringes and needles in pockets in their wet suits or in gear pouches.

"They took that on themselves, to administer essentially life-threatening anesthetic drugs to kids to keep them sedated enough to get them out of the cave, and I cannot tell you how impressed I am with those blokes," said Dr. Harry later.

John and Rick were in no doubt about the need for heavy sedation. Their experience trying to drag the four lost men through even five yards of sump showed just how essential it would be to render the boys immobile, if the plan was to have any hope of succeeding.

The last drug, atropine, was to reduce the amount of saliva in the boys' mouths. This would also be injected into their leg muscles. The divers knew that a leak in the seals of the full-face masks could be fatal, but the Australian doctor thought of something few had considered—that excess saliva could drool into the face masks and become a drowning hazard for the unconscious youths.

Dr. Harry had carefully considered the types of drugs and dosages that would be used, based on his years of experience and the advice of other experts. Still, he was not at all confident.

"Personally, I thought there was zero chance of success. I honestly thought there was no chance it would work," he would later admit. "So we set up a system for some feedback to come back after the first one or two kids, and if they hadn't survived that first sump, which was the longest one although not the most difficult one, then I was going to say, 'Well, that's all I can do,' [and] walk away at that point."

The dive option was the best chance the boys had for ever escaping that cave, but a rescue like this had never been attempted before, and this fact weighed heavily on the rescuers' minds. Amid all their preparations, they were also mentally preparing themselves for the very real possibility that something would go terribly wrong.

"The risk level was incredibly high," Major Hodges told the ABC's *Four Corners*. "When I was flat-out asked, 'What do you think the probability of success is?' I told the governor I thought maybe a 60 or 70 percent chance. So, I was fully expecting that we would, uh, accept casualties. Maybe three, four, possibly five would die."

The hardest job of transporting the boys was given to the British divers, who had had the most experience with cave rescues. Despite this, they, too, had serious doubts.

"It was [by] no means certain what the outcome would be," Rick later told ITV News.

Chris Jewell said it would be hard to invent such a difficult and dangerous operation.

"The scenario was almost a perfect storm of a rescue situation," he told Channel 5 News. "I couldn't quite believe that these boys had managed to get this far back into a cave. The sections that were flooded were flooded so significantly, it was a lot of diving we had to do. And that the water level wouldn't drop for months and months—it's really quite an incredible series of events, a situation to create; you almost couldn't write it. We didn't actually know at that point whether we could get them out alive."

20

LAST WORDS

On Saturday, July 7, the parents of the Wild Boars were called into a meeting. They were asked to leave their phones at the door. Inside were some of the most powerful figures involved in the operation. They told the parents that the conditions were favorable for a rescue attempt. The water level was stable. The boys had regained their strength. The parents were told their boys were learning how to scuba dive, although this wasn't actually the case. The boys would be taken out by some of the most experienced cave divers in the world. Everything was in place and ready. But they had to move now: the oxygen had lasted longer than expected, but was running out. And the next few days would be their last chance before the heavy rain forecast for Tuesday would completely flood the cave once again.

They needed the parents' authorization to go ahead with the rescue attempt. The parents were asked to sign a simple form, which was just a few lines in Thai. There was no letterhead. There were spaces where they could write in their names and their child's name. As well as requesting authorization, the form asked if the parents agreed to waive their rights in case something went wrong. There was no mention of sedation. They were not allowed to have a copy of the form or take a photo of it.

Naturally, the parents signed it.

That day, Jason Mallinson was diving in Tham Luang in order to familiarize himself with the route and deliver supplies. Considering the risk of the operation and the bleak predictions of success, he had an idea.

"I had a wet notes pad, which is a pad with waterproof paper, and I just thought, 'Here you are, write a message to your parents, write it on this pad and I'll take it out,'" he told the ABC's *Four Corners*.

Jason knew the parents would be thrilled to see their boys' handwritten messages. But also, if things didn't go to plan, these would represent the last words the boys said to their families.

"We never knew what was going to happen," he said. "We never knew that we were going to get them out. So, I thought it was important at least for them to be able to send a message out to their parents, maybe just to put their parents' minds at rest; to say, you know, 'I'm not doing too badly under the circumstances.'"

On white graph paper, specially treated so it could survive getting wet, one of the boys wrote in pencil a summary message in Thai on behalf of all them: "Don't worry about us. Everyone is healthy. We want to eat several types of food. When we get out we want to get home right away. Don't give us too much homework."

And then each boy and the coach penned their own messages in curly Thai script:

TITAN: "Mom and Dad, don't worry about me please, I am fine. Please tell Pee Yod, get ready to take me to eat fried chicken."

PONG: "Mom and Dad, I love you, please don't worry. I am safe now. Love you all."

NICK: "Mom and Dad, I love you, and I love *Nong* [*a Thai term for a younger sibling*] too. If I can get out, please take me to eat crispy pork. Love you Mom, Dad, *Nong*."

MARK: "Mom, are you well at home? I am fine. Please tell my teacher as well. Love you, Mom Nam Hom [*her name*]."

MIX: "Don't worry. I miss you all, Grandpa, Aunty, Dad, Mom, and *Nong*. I love you all. I am happy, the SEAL team is taking care of us very well. Love you all."

DOM: "I am fine. It is a bit cold, but don't worry. Please don't forget my birthday."

ADUL: "No need to worry about us anymore. I miss you all. I really want to go out so much."

NIGHT: "I love you, Mom and Dad. Please don't worry about me. I love you all."

TERN: "I miss you, Mom and Dad and [*illegible*]. I love you, Mom and Dad. Please don't worry. I can take care of myself."

NOTE: "I am safe, please don't worry. I love you, Mom, Dad, and everyone."

BIW: "Please don't worry, Mom and Dad. I have been gone for two weeks. I will come back and help you with the shop when I can. I will try to come soon."

TEE: "Mom, Dad, Brother, and Sister and family, please don't worry, I am very happy."

COACH EK: "Dear Aunty and Grandmother, I am fine, please don't worry about me too much. Please take care of your health. Please tell Grandmother to make crispy pork skin with dipping sauce for me. I will come and eat it when I get out. Love you all."

COACH EK: "Dear parents, we are all fine. The team is taking care of us very well. I promise that I will take the best care of the boys. Thanks for all your support and I apologize to all the parents."

The parents didn't blame Coach Ek. They were grateful for all he had done to keep their boys alive.

By Saturday, the Wild Boars team had been inside the cave for two weeks. The energy gels, food, and company had restored their strength, but the wait was dragging on. When the British divers had first popped up and told them the SEALs were on their way, the boys thought that meant they'd be getting out immediately. Five days later, they were well and truly ready to leave.

That day, some of the foreign divers went into the cave to give the Wild Boars the news that the rescue would be getting under way, and to give them a rundown of the plan. The divers told the boys that the plan was to sedate them and let the British cave rescue experts carry them out. The sedating procedure was explained to the children in a letter that Dr. Harry brought with him.

The letter, from one of the Thai doctors, explained to the children what the process would entail. "They were going to get a tablet which would make them feel funny. They would come down to the water, sit up on my lap. I was going to give them an injection in one leg, an injection in the other leg. They were going to go to sleep. They would wake up in bed," said Dr. Harry later. "When the Thai Navy SEAL read this out to the kids, I was watching their faces, and, honestly, they were just like, 'Yep, sounds like a plan.'"

Jason was also surprised by how well they accepted the news that they would be diving out—a prospect that would likely terrify most adults. "We told them about the plan, the vague details of a plan . . . how we'd have to dive them out, and none of them were whimpering or crying or anything. They just accepted what we were going to do. Really strong, you know, composure. Real mental strength from them, which was really surprising, considering their ages," Jason told the ABC's *Four Corners*.

That's exactly how Biw remembered the moment, too. Whatever it took to get out of that cave was fine by him.

"I'm coming out, I'm not afraid," Biw thought to himself.

21
D-DAY

Early on the morning of Sunday, July 8, an announcement was made over a loudspeaker: "For those in the media and anyone not involved in the operation, we politely ask that you leave this area."

All of the reporters and crews were asked to pack up and be off the mountain by 9 a.m. There were grumbles, for sure. Many of the larger networks had sunk considerable resources into setting up their "live spots" in the mud. It was obvious that the next designated media spot was not going to be as attractive as this one, with its view of the path leading to the cave.

The ABC's morning team packed up our (still unused) generator, umbrella, tables, and chairs and loaded it all into trucks to be taken down to the foot of the mountain and across the highway to the new press center—another cluster of canopies, this time outside a local government hall. There was a view of the misty mountains less than two miles away. It would have to do.

But the order to move away from the cave also signaled that something was happening. The rescue was surely about to start, speculated the journalists.

They were right.

"Today is D-Day," said the former governor of Chiang Rai, Narongsak Osottanakorn, at a press conference later that morning. "We are ready. The boys are ready and are strong enough to come out."

At around 8:20 a.m.—hours before the official announcement—the divers gathered for a briefing. There was little idle chatter. Nobody knew if they would finish the day as heroes or be dealing with dead children.

Together, they ran through the specifics of the plan once more. First, Dr. Harry would administer the sedation. Then, one of the four recovery divers—Rick, John, Chris, or Jason—would take an unconscious boy and transport him through the flooded parts of the cave.

The support divers would be stationed between sumps along the way to perform medical and equipment checks, and help carry the boy over dry sections and swim him through the floodwater. As well as the Euro team—Craig, Erik, Ivan, Mikko, and Claus—there would be two later additions to the rescue effort: an Englishman, Connor Roe; and Jim Warny, who was Belgian but lived in Ireland. Both were experienced cave rescue divers, but this would be Connor's first major rescue. They were deployed late and only just made it in time for the rescue, coming straight off a long flight and arriving just minutes before the first divers entered the cave.

The support divers would be divided into stations throughout the cave. Craig, Claus, and Mikko would be at Chamber 8;

Ivan and Erik would be at Chamber 6; and Connor and Jim would be at Chamber 5.

If things went according to plan, the recovery diver would hand over the boy to the US military team at Chamber 3, who would perform another medical check. Then he would be placed onto a rescue stretcher made from hardened plastic that could flex and glide over rocks. Among the rescuers it was known by its brand name, Sked (or Skedco)—a portmanteau of the words "skid" and "sled." Once the boy was strapped into the Sked, dozens of rescue workers from the United States, Australia, China, and Thailand would carefully maneuver the stretcher to the cave entrance. To get through the difficult rocky section between Chamber 3 and Chamber 2, the team from Chiang Mai Rock Climbing Adventures and the Americans had rigged up a zip-line system. The boy would be carefully hoisted up the steep incline and then lowered down the other side, all while strapped securely into the Sked.

Once at the cave entrance, the boy would receive more medical checks and a short ambulance ride to a field hospital just a few hundred yards away—two gray tents with waiting medical teams inside. If the medic gave the all clear, the boy would be loaded back into the ambulance and driven to the helipad at Ban Chong soccer field, for a chopper ride to Chiang Rai, where another ambulance would take him to a special quarantine ward that had been set up for the Wild Boars.

The briefing ended. There were more than one hundred people involved in the operation, and they all began their final preparations.

Around 10 a.m., the four recovery divers entered the cave. They were followed by Dr. Harry and the support divers.

The rescue operation had begun.

After about an hour, the divers reached Chamber 3—the base camp of the rescue.

At 11:50 a.m., the divers made their final gear checks and started leaving Chamber 3 for their respective posts, led by John, Rick, Jason, and Rob. They each had three cylinders, backup flashlights, their battered helmets, and preloaded ketamine syringes, needles not yet attached.

From this point on, there would be no communications back to Chamber 3: the divers would have to solve any crises on their own.

The US and Thai support teams watched the glow of the divers' lights fade away underwater. It would be five long hours before those left behind in Chamber 3 had any idea if the operation had been a success.

While they waited, the US military ran one last rehearsal, one that few people ever knew about.

Airman First Class Haley Moulton was tasked with carrying drinking water into the cave. Young and blond, she was petite in the real world, but next to some of her gym-buffed colleagues, she was positively tiny. It was only her second trip into the cave, and when she arrived in Chamber 3, she was given a new job.

"I got there and they're like, 'We need someone who's small,' so they can simulate the weight of who they're carrying out of the cave. And they were like, 'Oh, Moulton, you're doing it.'"

She was strapped into a Sked and told to try not to move while the rescuers hauled her through the dimly lighted passageways. It was going fine until they reached a steep section.

"I think it was the Australians who were managing that part. They pulled me up and my feet slipped through the bottom of the Skedco. So we had to stop and reset, and they found out they had to make the Skedco pretty tight, so that no one slips through."

It was a minor thing, but it could have been disastrous. The prospect of getting the boys out through the dangerous sumps only to drop them off a cliff onto the rocks was a scenario nobody wanted to imagine. It showed the thoroughness of the military-drilled organizers of the rescue. If it could be practiced, they'd test it. If it could be improved, they'd fix it.

But Airman First Class Haley Moulton faced something the boys—in their full-face masks—wouldn't have to worry about.

"I was just trying to keep my eyes closed, because their hands were going all over me, their muddy water was dripping on my face, and it was scary because my hands were strapped to my chest, so I couldn't move at all."

That part *would* be the same for the members of the Wild Boars. They'd be strapped in tight, completely dependent on those that passed them down the cave.

For the divers, the usual mode of communication using hand signals was out of the question in the soupy sumps. So Erik and Ivan—the two friends from Koh Tao—had come up with a simplified system: any time they reached an air pocket, the lead diver would wait for their buddy, have a quick chat to confirm everything was okay, and then continue on.

Ivan placed his borrowed helmet on his head and took the lead, submerging into the pool beyond Chamber 3, with Erik following. Almost immediately, things started to go wrong.

"Literally thirty seconds into the dive, my helmet—because it's so super buoyant—gets stuck in the cave on top of me and I don't feel it and I continue diving and . . ."

At this point during the retelling, Ivan tipped his head back slightly and made a choking sound.

"The one I borrowed was not a diving helmet, it was a climbing helmet, which has a lot of protective foam inside, which is incredibly buoyant, so it's not suitable for scuba diving."

With the helmet locked in place above and Ivan's momentum going forward, he was suddenly being choked by his chin strap.

"I'm like, shit, shit, shit. I can't move anywhere and I can feel that it's blocking my breathing . . . and I start to get sparks [in my eyes] because I don't get enough oxygen."

With one hand on the guide rope, his other hand fumbled with the latch.

"I can't get the f*cking thing open."

The methodical mind of the experienced technical diver went through the logic of breaking the first, most important rule of cave diving: never let go of the line. But the alternative was to die right then and there, choked by a floaty helmet with a tricky clasp.

"So, I let go of the line, get both my hands to the helmet, get the helmet off, get it free, put it back on again, and by this time the line is gone."

Adrift and blind, Ivan began a well-drilled emergency procedure. He stayed as still as possible and waved one extended arm up and down, circling deliberately, until he found the line again. He was lucky: it took only about forty-five seconds.

But in that brief time, Erik had swum by along the line, completely oblivious to the near-disaster. Both divers hauled themselves through the long, flooded tunnel, unaware that they'd switched positions.

When Erik popped up at the next air pocket, Ivan was no-where to be seen. Erik was baffled. They had only just started, and Ivan had been right there in front of him when the sump's murkiness cloaked them. Erik wondered if Ivan had somehow missed the big rock-climbing carabiner that indicated the place the line branched off from the loop. It was the *only* navigation point in the whole cave; it seemed impossible that Ivan could have missed it and continued around the big loop to reemerge in Chamber 3. Or maybe he had just skipped protocol and carried on without stopping for their appointed check-in. What should Erik do?

It was a quandary. Erik knew Ivan was a top diver who could get himself out of most trouble. Going backward on the line would risk bumping into other divers. It would also take time, and they were already a bit behind schedule. He had a job to do in Chamber 6. The boys and the rescue divers were depending on him to be there. So he swam on to the next chamber.

Seconds later, Ivan emerged in the same air pocket. He shone his light around the cave.

"I'm like, 'F*ck, where's Erik?'" he recalled. "'I know he thinks I'm in front of him, but he should have waited.'"

Presented with the same situation, Ivan then came up with a different conclusion.

"So I go back. It takes me about an hour to come all the way back to Chamber 3 and ask, 'Hey, is Erik here?'"

"No, he's with you," came the reply from the Americans.

"Ah, goddamnit," cursed Ivan.

Ivan changed his tanks and set off—again—from Chamber 3, through Chamber 4, past the laminated number 5 sign, and on into Chamber 6. There he found Erik. There was a long tense silence, Erik recalled. At least ten seconds went by as the two men just stared at each other.

It was a narrow miss, a mix-up that cost them time and dented their confidence. And the rescue hadn't even begun.

There was no time to waste talking about the mishap—they had a job to do. They began setting up their chamber, placing space blankets on the mud to create a working area and cable-tying LED lamps to the rocky ceiling. The dive instructors set out their fail-safes: backup regulators, spare tanks, food, rubber seals known as O-rings, and cable ties to repair broken hoses. (O-rings and cable ties are to divers what gaffer's tape is to landlubbers: they fix just about anything.)

Then Ivan and Erik sat on the muddy bank of their designated chamber and began the long wait for the first boy.

Outside the cave, there was much speculation about who would be brought out first.

There were two main schools of thought. Some believed the strongest boy would go first, as a test, to give the rescue workers the best chance of success. They could always adjust the plan after that. Others said it would be the weakest boy, because he'd need medical attention the most urgently.

In fact, the choice had nothing to do with the strength of the teammates.

"I talked with Dr. Harris," said Dr. Pak, who was caring for the boys inside the cave with the SEALs. "All of them are healthy, no complications whatsoever. Every one is more or less the same strength. We talked about how we are taking them out, the small one out first, or the bigger one, or other criteria. Dr. Harris told me, 'It doesn't matter who is out first.'"

So the question was put to the boys: whoever wants to go first, raise your hand. Many hands went up. Dr. Pak decided to delegate the decision to Coach Ek, the one who knew the boys best.

"The SEALs asked me to make that decision," explained Coach Ek. "So, [I decided] the first set would be those who come from Ban Wiang Hom, for the reason that they live farther away. What we planned was, once they were out, they would ride their bicycles home and let the other families know that the rest of the boys will be out tomorrow. And they would ask them to please cook some food for us."

The coach's reasoning showed how little the Wild Boars understood what was happening outside. They had no idea that their rescue had become the biggest news event in years and the whole world was transfixed by the dramatic operation.

The first four—Note, Tern, Nick, and Night—were chosen.

"I think it was their bravest guys that came out first," said Craig later.

Coach Ek said those who were not chosen weren't too disappointed. His words suggest that perhaps the boys remaining were just a little relieved not to be the guinea pigs in the high-stakes experiment.

"Those who are slower, when they see the post is filled, they just take their hand down. Actually, they all wanted to spend more time with the SEALs. At that time, we didn't really want to go out; we were very attached to them."

The Wild Boars had now been trapped for sixteen days. While they sat on that muddy ledge in the darkness lessened only by their flashlights, their plight had become the center of the world's attention. The media camped at the bottom of the mountain fed an insatiable demand from audiences and readers. Millions of people around the world were gripped by the story. Thousands of people had searched for them and for ways to get them out—soldiers, police, divers, climbers, construction workers, engineers, academics, mystics, and passionate volunteers. Now the world's best cave divers were going to attempt a rescue that had never been tried before.

Would they get out alive?

It all came down to this moment.

Note was the first Wild Boar to go. The fourteen-year-old was already wearing a wet suit, a welcome layer of warmth in the cool cave. But the wet suits were ill-fitting, and hypothermia remained a real risk during the several hours they would spend in and out of the water. Note swallowed the antianxiety tablet and started to feel relaxed.

"We got the Navy SEALs up the top of this hill just to sort of put [the boys] around the corner and get them sitting down, so they weren't watching what was happening to their mate," Dr. Harry later explained.

Note walked down the slope to Dr. Harry and sat in his lap. The Australian anesthetist was known for his calm, reassuring bedside manner. He prepared two syringes and eased them into each of Note's legs. Note was quickly unconscious.

He was then put into the rest of his diving gear—a buoyancy vest, the modified harness with a handle on the back, and an air tank strapped to his front. They chose not to use helmets for the boys because it interfered with the fit of the masks, but they placed packing foam inside their wet-suit hoods to give their heads some protection. The air was turned on and the all-important full-face mask was fitted. The divers carefully checked and rechecked the silicone seal to make sure it was tight against Note's face. It took about thirty seconds for Note to start breathing normally through the face mask.

Then, they did something that wasn't revealed to the public. They tied cable ties around Note's wrists and clipped them behind his back. It was a final measure to secure the child and make sure that if he *did* wake up from his ketamine slumber, he wouldn't try to rip off his face mask, endangering both his life and that of his rescue diver. It must have felt strange to handcuff the sleeping boy, but it was for his own good.

Then it was time for Dr. Harry to do the final check—a nerve-racking leap of faith.

"When I did my first test of pushing their face in the water—which . . . feels very wrong, I can tell you, the first time you do that—again about a thirty-second gap and they'd start breathing again."

Jason Mallinson volunteered to be the first recovery diver.

He took hold of the harness strap on Note's back and carefully submerged. He held the boy close, in roughly the same position as a tandem skydiver and their instructor, strapped together. Jason watched for bubbles in front of him as he began swimming cautiously through the first flooded tunnel.

As he recounted later, "So, with the diving, we'd submerge with the kid. And depending how the line lay, we'd either have them on the right-hand side or the left-hand side, either holding their back or holding their chest. I'd have a face here [gesturing just below his chin], depending if we were likely to hit the roof or not. Or if we could see what was going on, we'd hold them out a little bit farther. Swimming through the sump the first day, reasonable visibility, I could see sort of three feet in front of me."

The first dive was a long one, about 380 yards. When Jason surfaced in Chamber 8, Craig Challen was ready to do a quick medical check. Rick Stanton was also there. The divers were so unsure of whether the plan would work, they had arranged for a stop-and-check after the first boy. Rick had stayed in Chamber 8 so he could help with the first boy and then swim through with a message to Chamber 9, letting Dr. Harry know whether the child had survived the long dive.

Rick and Craig would help carry Note through the dry section. (Mikko and Claus were still on their way.) They brought Note out of the water and placed him on what they called a "drag stretcher," which they would use to transport him across to the next sump. The dry section was around 650 feet, long enough to require removing his diving gear. With the tank and lead weight, the boys were just too heavy to easily maneuver. And the divers didn't want to risk the heavy tanks bumping into the unconscious children and injuring them as they struggled over the rocks.

Craig checked Note's vital signs to ensure he was okay to continue. Satisfied that Note was stable, they placed his diving gear back on, again paying attention to his full-face mask, ensuring it was tightly sealed around his face.

Then Jason was on his own again, completely responsible for the life in his hands.

In the second sump, Jason felt his way along, avoiding bumping the boy into rocks at all costs. The two biggest dangers underwater were Note waking up and panicking, and his mask leaking. It wouldn't take much water to turn that plastic and silicone bubble of life into a death trap.

He passed through the narrowest restriction of the whole dive. Outside, the media—myself included—had been told the gap was just fifteen inches and reported that to our audiences. It became a factoid that resonated widely. Imagine squeezing through a hole just barely bigger than your head. But I learned long afterward that that was a mistake—the measurement for a restriction some divers had taken in error, which was actually for a side passage. In fact, the smallest choke point was located near Pattaya Beach and was less than a yard high, probably more like twenty-four inches. Considering the boy had a tank strapped to his front, that left little room for error.

Preventing the mask from becoming dislodged was a constant concern. The route was perilous. There were stalactites and rocks in their path, and another tricky point where the tunnel went vertical.

Jason's description later to the ABC's *Four Corners* vividly captured the treacherousness:

> You don't remember where the vertical section is, and the only time you find out about it is when your head bangs against the wall there. And you're trying to get yourself through this vertical section, but you can't remember exactly how it's laid out. So, I'm trying to get myself through it, but I'm also trying to get a kid through it, who's sort of horizontally in the water. Trying to post him through—no, that doesn't work; pull him back. Trying to post myself through—that doesn't work. And you could spend several minutes at . . . just one obstacle to try and find your way through. And you know, eventually we did it, but it's a very slow process and quite, quite daunting.

Protecting the child often meant taking a hit himself. The recovery divers all talked about bashing their helmets again and again into the cave ceiling, and using their bodies to provide a fleshy cocoon around their charges. And all the time, Jason and the other divers had to remember that number one rule of cave diving: "The main thing is, you've always got to keep in contact with that guideline. If you lose the guideline, you're in a lot of trouble."

Erik and Ivan had been waiting for hours in the cold of Chamber 6, the halfway point between the boys and the command center at Chamber 3.

With the chamber just barely illuminated by the hanging lights, they turned off their headlamps so they could watch for the telltale glow in the water that would signal the arrival of the first boy and his British transporter.

After what seemed a very long time, the water began to glow yellow, getting stronger as the light neared the surface. Then a dark silhouette emerged from the water. It was Jason. He was moving slowly—too slowly, thought Erik.

The Canadian peered into the darkness, trying to work out what that slowness meant. To him, it could be one of two things: "Things are either fine and there's no point rushing, or there's no point rushing because I can't change the situation; we're f*cked."

As Jason and the motionless boy came closer, Erik could start to make out more details. Ivan was already in the water, wading toward the diver and his precious package.

"I ran closer and I could now see that the kid's face was still in the water and everything is black, dark, hard to see, but I could see bubbles coming out from the regulator. That's all I needed to see: that means the kid is breathing and is alive," said Ivan.

"This is actually working," thought Erik.

The calmness with which Jason moved and spoke left a lasting impression on Erik.

"When I say 'stone cold,' I mean that in a completely positive way," he explained. "Maybe 'focused' is a better word to use. . . . The precise movements of someone with that much skill level . . ." Erik shook his head in amazement. "There wasn't one ounce of panic or hurry."

Ivan took hold of the boy and swam him on the surface toward their space blanket de-gearing station. Once Erik and Ivan were near the bank, they inflated Note's buoyancy vest to get him upright and onto the land. There, they removed his mask, tank, and harness. They ran through the medical checklist: breathing, saliva levels. Everything looked good.

"Slowly, slowly, take it easy," Ivan murmured to the boy in Thai, but it wasn't clear if he heard a thing.

After putting Note's gear back on, they checked the full-face mask. Usually this would take five seconds, but the men spent more than a minute making sure the seal was perfect, with no gaps or strands of hair under the double skirt of soft silicone. They knew that if they got this wrong, the kid would die.

Satisfied, the three divers slowly swam with Note to the other side of the chamber, a little over two hundred yards away. Ivan guided Note through the water to allow Jason as much rest as possible, saving his energy for the next dive.

"Are you good?" asked Ivan as he handed Note over to Jason.

"Yeah, I'm good," said Jason.

"Good luck," said Ivan.

Then Jason and Note disappeared underwater, quickly consumed by the brown murk.

"Awesome," Ivan remembers thinking. "One kid, alive, everything looked swell, no problems, all the equipment's working. Okay, what do we do now? Well, we wait."

Methodically, Jason carried Note through the rest of the flooded cave, diving and wading. He stopped at Chamber 5, where Connor and Jim assisted. Chamber 4 had spare cylinders stashed but was unmanned. Jason carried on. The dive between Chamber 4 and Chamber 3 was particularly tricky, with plenty of pipes and cables to snag on.

Once at Chamber 3, Jason's job was done. At around 4:50 p.m., he handed Note over to the US military team to do a medical check. All good. The boy was loaded onto the stretcher. The Chiang Mai rope team pulled him up to the top of what Chinese rescue worker Li Shuo called the "little mountain." The Sked traveled along the zip line, down to the American and Chinese men below. Vern was there to help, too.

At first, Li Shuo was worried. He didn't think the child was breathing. He felt frightened. But he soon realized there was breath, though it was slowed by the drugs, and difficult to notice in the tense moment.

As Note was passed along, one man stayed by his side, a member of the rock-climbing team called Toto. Even though the boy was unconscious, Toto whispered encouragements to him as he was carried out.

"You're almost there . . . keep it up . . . you've come so far . . . your big brothers are here to look after you," whispered Toto.

The rescue workers used the large orange water pipes installed in the cave as a rail for the hard plastic stretcher to slide on, carefully guiding it over the boulders. "We had to use a rope system to pull the boy's stretcher through this narrow section. We had to sit on the rocks to pull the rope in order to get the boy's stretcher through," said Li Shuo.

From the end of the zip line to the entrance, the terrain varied. The stretcher was carried, floated through a three-yard sump, carried, floated through a ten-yard sump, and passed on again. There were more than a hundred people involved in this high-stakes game of pass-the-parcel; one slip of a rescuer's boot could bring the whole thing undone. At every moment, arms stretched out, waiting to carry or to catch Note.

This was truly an international effort, with the boy lifted to freedom by rescuers from Australia, the United Kingdom, Finland, Denmark, Canada, Belgium, the United States, Thailand, China, Singapore, and possibly other countries. Political and personal tensions dissolved in the darkness as the big messy world focused down to one thing: keeping that boy alive.

"Once he was handed over to us, we were down at his face mask, just listening for that breath," said Senior Constable Matthew Fitzgerald of the Australian Federal Police. "He was breathing. There was instant relief."

All the while, Note lay unconscious on his stretcher. The full-face mask remained on, and an air tank was strapped into the stretcher, pumping the special mix of oxygen-rich air. As he reached the entrance of the cave and was passed over to the Thai medics, a cheer went up among the rescue workers. This cheer spread backward, like a wave, through the tunnel—a moment of happiness and relief.

They'd done it.

Now just twelve more to go.

22
THREE MORE BOYS

Fourteen-year-old Tern had watched his schoolmate Note go bravely down the hill; now it was his turn. The injections knocked him out quickly, and he was geared up for the dive. This time, John Volanthen would have the momentous task of guiding the boy through the most dangerous sections of the cave. For days, John had been mentally getting ready for a truly horrible scenario.

"I was prepared to take a live child underwater and bring out a corpse," he said.

And yet John also had a conflicting thought that was even stronger.

"I was 110 percent determined that *my* child was going to survive."

He descended into the water, holding Tern close.

Once John and Tern had disappeared, Dr. Harry realized something: he'd forgotten to wait for the all clear from Rick before sending Tern. He paused the operation in Chamber 9 until he had word from Rick.

In fact, Rick was already swimming up the long, flooded tunnel toward Dr. Harry. As he made his way up the passage, he was surprised to bump into John going down, carrying a boy. They carefully moved around each other underwater, allowing John to carry on toward Chamber 8, and Rick to dive on to Chamber 9. Rick emerged and passed on the positive news to the Australian doctor: the first boy—Note—had gone through fine; their plan seemed to be working.

In Chamber 6, Erik and Ivan were cold.

"The first thirty minutes, we were active," said Ivan. "[Then] absolutely freezing."

The first two boys had come through with no major problems. Ivan and Erik helped replace the divers' air tanks if needed, and sent them on their way.

Then they waited. And waited. They had no idea that Dr. Harry had paused the operation at Chamber 9.

In the cold, dark doubts emerged.

"All the maybes, possibilities, what-ifs—all that started to surface," said Ivan. "When everything becomes silent and you're not preoccupied with a job, you start to think about, 'Oh my god, they're coming out, do you think they're going to be alive?' Every minute you wait, you start to be, 'Oh f*ck, they f*cked up, something's gone wrong. Why are they not here? Mate, it can't take them three hours to gear them up. What happened?' You're very aware of every little sound."

There were numerous false alarms. The two men would hear something and jump up with pulses racing, only to realize it was nothing, sit back down on the muddy bank, and resume their chilling wait, eyes trained on one end of the black pool.

"I thought [the chances of success] were high . . . other-wise I would not have participated in it. But not 100 percent. In the back of my head, there was the risk that maybe not everybody would make it," said Ivan. "They were very long hours."

Despite everyone's fears, the first two boys—Note and Tern—appeared to be doing okay, Note completely, and Tern at least as he went through the first sump.

Next, Nick was called down.

Unbeknown to him, photos of the Wild Boars, taken from their social media accounts, were being circulated around the globe. Nick had drawn the short straw: the one of him used by almost everyone was an unflattering shot. His eyes were closed and his head tilted on an angle, with his index fingers pressed into each cheek—a pose more befitting a cutesy female K-pop starlet than a fifteen-year-old boy. It was the sort of thing that most teenagers would be highly embarrassed about, but as it was, he had no idea. And considering all he'd been through, he probably wouldn't have cared anyway.

Dr. Harry gave him his injections, and Nick was strapped into his diving gear. Then Rick took over.

"They were basically a package with a handle, like a shopping bag," Rick would later tell ITV in the United Kingdom. "We're used to transporting all sorts of things underwater, but to trans-port a human life is about the ultimate responsibility."

Rick took the handle on the back of the harness, holding the boy close, as the other recovery divers had done. Like them, he wanted to be able to see, hear, and feel the bubbles coming from the full-face mask, and he wanted *his* head and *his* body to hit the rocks, not Nick's. Underwater, he reached out his other hand for the guide rope and started the journey out.

Mark had been eager to leave in the first group, but the rescue team couldn't find a mask small enough for him. Even though he was two years older than the youngest, Titan, he was tinier. He would have to wait another night in the cave.

Night would go next instead. He swallowed his tablet of alprazolam and walked down the slope to the Australian doctor.

So far, the rescue was going well. Dr. Harry was relieved the drugs appeared to be working. But there was always a nervous moment as the anesthetist put the boy's body into a state between life and death. Each time a sedated boy entered the water, he would stop breathing for about thirty seconds.

Night sat on the doctor's lap, as the other three boys had done. The two injections went into his legs. But this time there was a problem. Night had a chest infection—possibly early stages of pneumonia. His breath became irregular. He was reacting badly to the drugs.

"He was oversedated," said Dr. Harry. "I ended up lying on a bit of sand with him for half an hour, sort of spooning him, I guess, holding his airway open, thinking, 'This is what I predicted was going to happen.'"

After about thirty minutes, the boy started to recover.

"He sort of fired up," said Dr. Harry, adding with a laugh, "and needed another dose to put him back in the water about 200 yards down the track."

It was Chris Jewell who took hold of Night.

"The boys were extremely brave," said Chris, in a later interview with the United Kingdom's 5 News. "They did everything right in order to make it possible for us to be able to rescue them. From when they were first trapped in the cave, conserving their light for the nine days until they were found, all the way through to how they acted when we started the operation. I never saw a whimper or a tear in the eye, extremely calm, very brave, and really strong, determined young men."

But the boys had the benefit of not fully understanding the risks—of which Chris and the other recovery divers were all too aware.

"We knew that any attempt we made would have a probability of not total success. We had a probability of losing one of the boys, ultimately. And there was some pressure on us obviously because of that."

As they emerged, the four boys were taken by ambulances from the cave mouth to the field hospital. They were checked by doctors and then put back in the ambulances and driven down the hill to a flat piece of land. If the boys hadn't been so groggy, they might have recognized the place: the Ban Chong soccer field, where they had played their friendly match fifteen days earlier. They'd come full circle.

Helicopters stood waiting. As each new ambulance approached, the blades of one of the choppers would start roaring, and the back lowered to form a ramp. Half a dozen bent-over figures then carried each stretcher across the grass in a half run.

One by one, over the course of several hours, the choppers rose up, banked, and pointed their noses in the direction of Chiang Rai, where a special ward at Prachanukroh Hospital was waiting for the Wild Boars. There the doctors would run tests, checking first their breathing, and then looking for signs of hypothermia. But the doctors were also on the lookout for something known as "cave disease," an airborne lung infection spread by bat droppings. The doctors didn't know it yet, but there were no bats that deep inside Tham Luang. Like the upper reaches of Mount Everest, this was a death zone, where mammals such as bats and humans were not supposed to survive for long.

Just as the lack of communications beyond Chamber 3 made for an anxious wait for the American and Thai soldiers stationed there, the support divers also had little idea of what was happening elsewhere in the cave. They knew that each boy had been alive and well when he passed through their chamber. But then what?

After Chris had come through with Night, Erik and Ivan tidied up their workstation, ready for the next day's operation. They then put on their tanks and masks and began the dive out of the cave.

When they surfaced at Chamber 3, many eyes were watching them. Those on land knew that the divers needed a few moments to remove their masks and compose themselves before any news would sink in. US Captain Mitch Torrel let the silence hang even longer.

Ivan looked up at him from the water. There was no need to ask the question.

"Ivan, they're all fine," said Captain Torrel.

By 9 p.m., the day's operation was over.

"Today is the most perfect day," said rescue leader Narongsak Osottanakorn. He was facing a banked semicircle of cameras, tripods, and people at the new media hub at the bottom of the hill. "We've now seen the faces of members of the Wild Boars football team."

At the cave site, the divers and rescue workers gathered for debriefing sessions and to plan the next day's mission. There had been one heavy shower that evening, but the pumps had kept the water level stable.

For British diver Chris Jewell, there were mixed emotions. "There was a sense of euphoria mixed very heavily with a sense of—we were going to have to do this again, not just once but twice more. To go through the entire stressful process, start to finish, on at least two more occasions. The diving wasn't going to get any easier."

Sasivimon Yuukongkaew was one of the very few women to be inside the cave throughout the search and rescue. She was the wife of the SEALs' top commander and an administrator of its Facebook page.

That morning, she wanted to somehow capture this moment of united purpose, of international cooperation. She asked three of the SEALs to pose for a photo, just of their hands. Each hand grabbed hold of the wrist of another, forming a triangle. She took the photo with her phone. It was a nice image, but not quite right.

"I need a *farang* hand," she said, using the Thai word for Caucasian foreigners.

She asked a Thai staffer from the Australian embassy to find her "a white hand." Moments later a member of the Australian Federal Police rescue team, Sergeant Mark Usback, was brought over. He joined two of the SEALs, and the three locked hands. "Better," thought Sasivimon, but the Australian was the only one wearing a wedding ring. She asked him to take it off for the shot. He did. She took one last photo. That was it! Two Thai hands (wearing Kruba Boonchum's red bracelets) and an international hand with a sleeve of camouflage uniform showing, gripped together in a triangle of strength and cooperation.

"The photo I think encompasses the unity we all had during the rescue," said Sergeant Usback. "It sounds a little corny, but that's how it was. The ability for so many cultures to come together and work as one was pretty amazing."

For the Australian, the rescue would be the highlight of a thirty-year career in policing.

Sasivimon posted the image on the SEALs page, and it became iconic, shared across Thailand and the world.

As the operation wrapped up for the night, she wanted to let the public know they should rest easy and look forward to the next day. She posted on the SEALs Facebook page: "Sleep tight tonight everyone. Hooyah."

23

FIVE, SIX, SEVEN, EIGHT

That Sunday night, Ivan became ill. Still, he showed up to take his place in the rescue team on Monday, but his colleagues took one look at him and sent him to the medical tent. There, he was given an intravenous drip and sent home.

The dive team was one man down, so they changed the stations slightly. Jim Warny took Ivan's spot, joining Erik in Chamber 6, while another British diver joined Connor Roe in Chamber 5. Josh Bratchley had arrived the night before from his home in Devon, UK, where he worked as a meteorologist. He was an experienced caver and a member of the Devon Cave Rescue Organisation.

At the morning press briefing, the rescue commander was in a confident mood.

"We're 100 percent ready and expect everything to be completed faster than expected," said Narongsak Osottanakorn.

However, there was a very different attitude among the divers and those helping to plan the rescue.

"My concern was that we would become complacent," said Major Charles Hodges. "Because, yes, it was huge. I mean we just hit a home run. Four for four—you can't get any better than that. But in my mind the risk level didn't go down any at all."

The second day of rescues got under way at 11 a.m. Again, those with the farthest to swim into the cave went in first—Dr. Harry, Craig, and the four principal recovery divers: Rick, John, Chris, and Jason.

The success of the first day of rescues had surprised everyone involved. It seemed their plan was almost perfect. They made only small tweaks. They wrote each boy's name on his hand, so rescue workers could easily tell whom they were dealing with. They moved some air tanks around inside the cave. And they decided that it was not necessary to keep the full-face mask on once the boys had finished the diving part and reached the Chamber 3 base camp safely. As much as the full-face mask was a lifesaver underwater, it could quickly become a death trap if there was any problem with the air supply from the tank while the boys were in the hands of non-divers.

There was one annoying hurdle to overcome the morning of that second rescue day, a technical one. The British divers had researched Thailand before they arrived and learned that the standard connection between the regulator hose and the air tank was an A-clamp. They brought adaptors and had been using them successfully for several days. But on that Monday morning, they arrived to find that the cylinders laid out for the rescue were fitted with an alternative connection, known as a DIN system. It wasn't a catastrophe, but it meant they had to take valves from other tanks and fit them to the filled tanks. It was frustrating and a waste of time.

There would be frustration, too, for little Mark, two and a half miles inside the cave. Once again, he was eager to go with the second lot, but again he was thwarted. The rescuers still couldn't find a full-face mask small enough to seal over his tiny face.

Mix went first, with Jason. Adul was carried out by John. Third to go was Biw, in the hands of Chris. And Rick took the last boy out that day, team captain Dom.

Each one of the boys had to be resedated during the rescue, some of them twice. Several of the British divers held advanced first-aid qualifications that allowed for the administration of morphine, so giving the intramuscular injection wasn't too far beyond what they'd been trained to do. John kept his predosed syringes in a pouch on one of his air tanks. When the child started to stir, he would stop, attach the needle to the syringe, and inject it through the boy's wet suit into his leg.

On the second day of the rescues, when John was halfway through his dive with Adul, there was a problem.

"Every time we put this kid's head underwater, he stopped breathing and he wouldn't start breathing," said John. "It took a number of attempts over about fifteen, twenty minutes to get this child to breathe underwater—realizing he wasn't breathing, getting him out of the water, into the recovery position, getting him breathing . . . there was a cycle until we [John and Josh] were comfortable that he was properly breathing, the mask was on and sealed, and I was okay to carry on."

Jason Mallinson had a close call with one of his patients. (It's not clear which day or which boy was involved.) As he was swimming through a partially flooded passage with no bank, the boy started to wake up. Jason kept his syringes in his wet-suit pocket and had to try to get one out and fit a needle, while also controlling the child in the water.

"It was very tricky. I had syringes floating around on the surface, just trying to grab hold of 'em," Jason told the American Broadcasting Company.

Fortunately, the boys remembered none of these perilous moments. The ketamine had a strong "dissociative" effect, meaning their thoughts were disconnected from their physical reality.

For Biw, his mind went on a magical journey during the rescue. Once Dr. Harry gave him his sedative, the dark cave world quickly became even darker as the ketamine took effect. He stopped moving, but his mind lit up.

"I dreamed that King Rama IX [the revered King Bhumibol] held my hand and the hands of the other three boys and he sent us off on a helicopter."

The first Wild Boar that day emerged from the cave at around 4:45 p.m., meaning the extraction went faster than the previous day. As before, the ambulances ferrying the Wild Boars raced to the helicopters. Huge white parasols were held up around the choppers to keep long-lens photographers from snapping pictures as the boys were loaded up the ramp. In Chiang Rai, another ambulance shuttle took each boy to the same hospital ward as the others. Local residents lined the streets to cheer as the ambulances went by.

Once again, every time the media announced another successful rescue, there was a feeling of relief and joy around the world.

The bird's-nest collectors of Libong Island tried until the end. Even after learning of the rescue of the first four boys from the cave, that Monday they still hiked back up the mountain. While the world waited for news of the second round of rescues, the men lowered themselves once again into dark holes of unknown depth, just in case there was another, less risky option for extracting the Wild Boars.

Over the twelve days they had been in Chiang Rai, they had explored dozens of shafts. Some ended after just 130 feet; others wound down through the limestone and granite for hundreds of yards, but ultimately they all turned out to be dead ends.

"That longest descent might have got them close," thought Rawheen Joanglao. Could it have been the shaft that once illuminated Pattaya Beach into a dazzling aqua-blue pool? Was it possible the dead end at the bottom was merely a plug of fallen sticks, soil, and rocks?

The bird's-nest collectors would never know. When they came down from the mountain that day to find that another successful rescue had taken place and eight boys were now free, they decided to stop. They flew back to Libong Island, a journey taking them from the top mountainous corner of Thailand to the tropical south; from the dark confines of unexplored sinkholes to the turquoise seas of their home.

They had achieved no great glories. But they had tried their hardest. And they had risked their lives, dangling precariously from their single ropes, probing the crust of the earth for a way through. Somewhere below them, the boys and Coach Ek had been waiting; indeed, some were waiting still for that last rescue. But now it was time for Rawheen to go home, where his three children waited for their own father.

Mix, Adul, Biw, and Dom joined their teammates Note, Tern, Nick, and Night in the hospital. They were placed behind glass in a sterile ward and restricted to a bland hospital diet at first. This was a considerable disappointment: the SEALs had been vague about arrangements once they left the cave, and the boys had just presumed they'd be eating home-cooked food and sleeping in their own beds.

"In the morning, they complained about being hungry and asked for *kao pad krapao*," reported Governor Narongsak.

It was a good choice—a classic dish of Thai comfort food, available from street vendors and restaurants across the country: minced meat, usually pork or chicken, flavored with holy basil, fired up with chilies, and served with steamed rice.

Later that night—much later—as Jum and I got an order in before our hotel kitchen closed, I decided I too wanted *kao pad krapao* for dinner. So did Jum. When I looked around, almost everyone had ordered the dish. The next day, I'd find out that the same had happened at restaurants across Mae Sai. In a spontaneous act of solidarity, everyone was eating the delicious rice dish that the boys craved.

Little Mark was also dreaming of food from home.

He was severely disappointed: he had been first in line for the rescues, eager to get out; but for two days now he had been left sitting on the bank of Nern Nom Sao. He longed desperately for comfort food, especially the rice congee that Thais call *joke*.

That night, Dr. Pak heard Mark talking in his sleep.

"I want *joke*, I want *joke*," muttered the thirteen-year-old as he slept on the mud.

24

CLOSING WINDOW

For days, the weather had been kind. There had been some showers, but nothing substantial. John had been tracking the water level deep inside the cave. On the first two rescue days, he had brought a bottle of water in to drink when he reached Chamber 9. He placed the empty bottle in the silt at the water-line each day and so could tell that the water level was dropping steadily. John—like Vern—didn't think the pumps were having much effect beyond Chamber 3, but they both thought the creek diversions on top of the mountain were probably helping. That, and the lack of rainfall, were allowing the sumps to drain into the rock and out the cave entrance.

But on Tuesday, July 10, that was all likely to change.

All week, the weather forecasters had been warning of heavy storms approaching—the sort of monsoonal downpour that had trapped the team in the cave in the first place; the sort that could push the divers back again, leaving the Wild Boars, the SEALs, and Dr. Pak stuck in an airless pocket two and a half miles inside a mountain. If they couldn't get them out before the storm hit, Chamber 9 would likely entomb them.

"Today is probably the last weather window—and it isn't a big window," said caver Martin Ellis, in a report published later on his caving blog.

There had been a lot of speculation over whether the divers would again bring four people out, leaving one in the cave alone for another day. But the weather made that impossible. The divers reconfigured and would attempt to bring out all five. When Governor Narongsak announced this decision at Tuesday morning's press conference, the crowd broke out into applause.

Among the divers and the Americans, there was little celebration. The fact that they had saved eight children didn't reduce the pressure. If anything, the public's growing sense that this operation was a "done deal" only heightened the tension.

"It was clear from the first day that whatever Harry was doing worked, the sedation worked. So going forward, any children that didn't survive, it was clearly down to that diver making a mistake," said John. "We haven't been lucky, we've been very careful; but the risks are still the same."

Overnight it had rained heavily, and it was still raining as the divers arrived that morning.

"Both Rick and I were very concerned as we'd seen how ferociously the water in the cave could rise. The other British divers hadn't been there at high water," said John. "We were also concerned that if the cave flooded, we would be the farthest from the entrance, and so at the back of the queue to exit—behind Thai special forces, American soldiers, and brawny Australians—we knew we weren't going to fight our way to the front. That all felt a bit edgy."

The recovery and support divers held their usual prerescue briefing outside the cave. Dozens of gleaming silver cylinders were lined up, all filled with air or the 80 percent oxygen mix and ready to go. But again, despite the previous day's explanation, they were fitted with DIN valves, which all had to be changed to A-clamp systems before they could be used in the rescue.

At 10:08 a.m., the final mission began.

It was Coach Ek who went first on the final rescue day. His face had become gaunt, totally changing his appearance. For eighteen days, he'd kept the boys calm and together in the darkness, teaching them meditation, encouraging them to conserve energy.

The task of taking the coach out was given to Jim Warny, the experienced Belgian cave diver who lived in Ireland. He had taken Ivan's place, and joined Erik in Chamber 6 on the second day of the rescue, but this would be his first time swimming out with an immobile body bubbling away in the sump water. Erik was left to manage Chamber 6 single-handedly for the final rescue day.

John took Tee, the oldest of the players.

He had a scary moment as he dived between Chamber 4 and Chamber 3, the last sump before his part of the rescue was over. Being close to the cave command center, it held the remnants of many failed efforts to get power, phone, and oxygen lines through the tunnel.

"There was so much debris in the passage—and bear in mind, visibility is a few inches. I was quite close to the exit of the sump and my child stopped moving," said John.

Tee was snagged on something in the cave.

"I had to park him—literally leave him on the bottom [of the flooded cave]. I'm tethered to him so I can't lose him. I clipped myself to the line, so I don't lose the line. Then I've got to feel down the child to find out what's obstructing him and why I can't pull him forward. I find a black telephone wire . . . cut the black telephone wire, free it from his legs, then move back up to reconnect with the line, reconnect with the child, and then move off again."

John said this incident confirmed for him the value of sedation. There's little chance a conscious person would have been able to keep calm and stay still if they became entangled and their rescue diver left them on the cave floor.

The youngest and second-smallest boy, Titan, went next. He was a bit intimidated by the big Australian doctor, who looked like a giant to him. He sat on Dr. Harry's lap.

"Are you okay?" asked Dr. Harry.

Titan nodded.

When the injection went in, Titan nodded again, but this time his head didn't rise. He was out almost instantly. He remembered nothing of the journey out. None of the boys did. Dr. Harry's potions were spot-on.

Chris—who by now had done the underwater obstacle course twice—had the job of taking Pong, one of the quieter boys, out of the cave.

At 4:37 p.m., they were felt on the dive line by those in Chamber 3. "Fish on the line," shouted one of the Americans. But around 5 p.m., they could no longer be detected.

Just a few hundred yards away, underwater, Chris had been switching grip, moving Pong from his left hand to his right hand, when he lost the line. He was in the same difficult dive section between Chamber 4 and Chamber 3, where John had just freed Tee from the black telephone line. Like John, he was tethered to the boy, but they were adrift and blind.

"At this point, I hadn't moved. I knew the dive line couldn't be far away, but I couldn't find it," Chris would later tell the United Kingdom's Channel 5 News.

His first reaction was that of an experienced cave diver and a man with immense composure.

"I deliberately tried to slow my breathing down, stay exactly where I was, stay stationary, deploying a strategy of looking for the line and then ultimately finding this electrical cable."

The electrical cable led him back to the unmanned Chamber 4, where spare cylinders and other equipment were stashed.

"Once I realized where I was, it was a relief. Obviously, I had one of the children with me, I still needed to get him out to safety; hypothermia is a concern when you've got a young child in the water for that length of time. So I wrapped him up in a space blanket while I waited for one of my diving colleagues to come past," he said.

After a while, Jason swam past with his boy, the final one. Dr. Harry was behind them. He stopped, checked on Pong, and spoke to Chris. They decided that Dr. Harry would take Pong for the final sump, with Chris following close behind.

It was a near miss. But thanks to the calmness of Chris and the helping hand of Dr. Harry, another boy was at the Chamber 3 base camp. Another Wild Boar was saved.

Poor little Mark. Each day he had waited, desperate to get out of the miserable cave. But each day, his escape had been thwarted. Overnight, Pae had found a smaller-sized silicone skirt to fit another brand of full-face mask. It was pink. He still wasn't 100 percent sure it would be the right fit, but there was no more time to wait; they'd have to give it a go.

Mark got his injections and went to sleep in his tiny wet suit. Jason checked the pink-skirted full-face mask. It only just formed a seal around Mark's small face. But there was no other option. They'd have to risk it and be extra careful not to bump him against a rock and flood his breathing apparatus—a task that had become even more challenging now that the visibility in the sumps was approaching practically zero, churned up by the day's traffic.

"I was confident of getting the kid out; I wasn't 100 percent confident of getting him out alive," Jason later told the ABC's *Four Corners*.

As it turned out, Mark was in safe hands. Just before 6 p.m., Jason emerged with him into Chamber 3. Minutes later, Dr. Harry followed with Pong. They handed the boys over to the rescue workers, who strapped them into rescue stretchers and began passing them through the cave. Around 7 p.m., the last boy reached the cave entrance.

All thirteen Wild Boars had been saved.

"[It was] quite emotional," said the usually "stone cold" Jason about the final walk out of the cave. "As we were getting closer and closer to the entrance, I got quite emotional. I don't normally; it's just, what we were doing has to come out. And I've got a kid myself now, so it was quite a good feeling."

The media spotters who'd snuck into key positions told the reporters down the mountain, who then told the world. Within minutes, elation spread across the globe. They'd done it! The boys and Coach Ek were alive and safe.

It was a fairy-tale ending.

But there would be one last drama before it was all over.

By around 6:30 p.m., the recovery divers and support divers had returned to Chamber 3, tired but thrilled by the successful rescue. However, the operation wasn't over until everyone was out safely.

All the foreign volunteers were experienced cave divers, but for the three SEALs and Dr. Pak, who had been in the cave with the Wild Boars for an entire week, the dive out from Chamber 9 was going to be a challenge. Over the last few days, the British divers had brought in supplies for each of them, including full cylinders and a mask. They told them to wait for two hours after the last boy went out and then begin their exit dive. The rescue coordinators couldn't quite celebrate until they were out.

While the fifty or so rescue workers at the Chamber 3 base camp—including Thai SEALs, US military, and the support divers—waited for the final four to arrive, they started packing up their gear, getting ready to haul it out of the cave. There were fast-food burgers and fried chicken to eat and—once the last Wild Boar had left the cave—a bottle of American whiskey was shared around.

Around 9 p.m., two of the SEALs arrived in Chamber 3. Then a third. Finally, the fourth and final member of the Thai team popped up. Everyone was greatly relieved—now they could relax.

By this stage, the tricky S-bend separating Chambers 3 and 2 had been partially drained by the pumps, so non-divers could get through. But just as the last SEAL reached the safety of Chamber 3, a pipe attached to a water pump burst. Water started to rapidly fill the S-bend. Within minutes, they would all be trapped.

"I don't know if it was kind of a supernatural intervening, but one of the pumps back at Chamber 3 failed, and we had a fair amount of guys out there, waiting for the last group of SEALs to come out," said Master Sergeant Derek Anderson. "We got the call, 'Hey, water levels are rising fast.' That was definitely a spike of adrenaline toward the end of the night."

Everyone hurried to squeeze themselves through the cork-screw exit. There was no time to bring equipment. The Americans, SEALs, and other support workers dropped what they were doing and dashed for the exit. They made it out with minutes to spare.

Just before 7 that night, I pushed my earpiece into my ear, clipped the cable to the back of my collar, and straightened myself in the pool of TV lights. We were minutes away from going live to Australia for the big update—the one we'd all been waiting for.

Jum was nearby, out of shot. All night, she'd been feeding me the developments. She had three sources and when all three agreed, she'd let me know. Sometimes I could hear other networks announcing, "One more out," but until Jum told me it was confirmed, it wasn't. Finally, her sources said all the team were out. But after a misinformation debacle on day one of the rescues—Reuters had reported that six boys had been rescued, which we'd dutifully relayed to our audience, only to find out soon after that this information was incorrect—we really wanted to be sure.

At 6:47 p.m., the Thai Navy SEALs Facebook page posted an update, which the app translated to English as: "Twelve wild pigs and coaches out of the cave. Safe everyone. This time, waiting to pick up 4 Frogs." "Frogs" meant frogmen—a reference to the SEAL divers still in the cave.

"Yes," said Jum, smiling. "Oh, now I need to give someone a hug. After this cross."

"One minute to you," said the voice in my earpiece.

"Hang on," I said, "I have to go and hug my producer." I jumped off-camera to give Jum a quick embrace.

As I started the live remote, I found myself filled with a huge surge of emotion. Gone was the careful neutral face of the professional reporter. I was grinning ear to ear. I told the audience the wonderful news, feeling the happiness building. Suddenly, happiness was becoming something else. I felt my throat getting tighter, tears welling up in my eyes. I got through the remote, but only just.

We worked all night, doing regular live remotes and radio interviews for eighteen hours straight. That sort of interest from the network was unprecedented in all our careers.

On the mountain, there were jubilant scenes of celebration. Support workers lined up in two rows at the path to the cave to cheer and yell "Thank you" as each of the divers and rescue workers walked out. At the SEALs camp, it was party time. The men sang and danced and whooped.

The parents asked Josh Morris if he could find the British divers and translate for them, so they could thank them in person. The two groups came together, and Josh started to relay their heartfelt words to the UK team. Mark's mother came forward with a "crazy-intense" thank-you, that Josh remembers like this:

"I was so worried about him. He's so little I didn't think he'd be able to make it. He's going to be weak this whole time. And then he didn't come out on the first day, he didn't come out on the second day, and then he was the last person to come out on the third day, and I thought, 'Oh no, is he alive?' But I couldn't be happier."

For the American in the middle, it was an overwhelming moment.

"I kinda cried in the middle of it. I had to stop, and John patted me on the shoulder and said, 'Thank you,' and I finished."

The parents *wai*'d the rescuers, and the two sides stepped forward to hug each other.

For John Volanthen, it was a nice moment, but the veteran rescue diver was a long way from tears.

"[When] we meet the parents, usually it's to say, 'I'm very sorry for your loss.' It's always emotionally charged. For me, it was just a relief this time that we didn't have to look anyone in the eye and say, 'I'm sorry for your loss.'

"I am quite a lot less emotional about this than perhaps the press would like. What I would say . . . is, Who would you rather come rescue you? Someone who can make unemotional, sensible decisions and then stick by them and execute the plan? Or someone who is a much more emotional type of person? The emotion doesn't work. It's quite hard—I just am what I am.

"It wasn't a miracle. It was a lot of people working very hard and a lot of people pushing. . . . There were a lot of very carefully considered steps to make that happen."

That evening's press conference was huge. Governor Narongsak wore his blue volunteer's cap and yellow neckerchief.

Several soldiers were with him. They made their way to a table in front of the waiting media and arranged themselves in a line. Then, for a moment, they just stood there, as the press corps erupted into applause. For ten seconds, fifteen seconds, they let it wash over them, accepting the praise on behalf of everyone who had worked so tirelessly.

"Nobody thought we could do it; it was a world first," said Narongsak, once they sat down. "It was Mission Possible for Team Thailand. This mission was successful because we had power. The power of love. Everybody sent it to the thirteen.

"We'd like to thank the world and the Thai people. We've brought all the five out safely [today]. Their relatives are now going to take a fresh shower and get to see them at hospital through glass [windows]."

There were more cheers and applause as the press conference wrapped up. I didn't have to file immediately, so I wandered around for a few minutes, trying to sear the scene—and the feelings—into my memory. These moments didn't come often.

Not long after, I bumped into a couple of reporters I knew from Bangkok and Phnom Penh. They were just as astounded by the result.

"It's just amazing," we said, in different ways, over and over again, shaking our heads, grinning, and admitting to each other that none of us had dared hope it would end so well. "It's just amazing."

It was little wonder this story had touched the hearts of so many people around the world. It had it all: a misadventure we could all relate to; children trapped and hungry; the race against time; the water rising, falling; the world sending its best and bravest; the tragedy of an unexpected death; then the dramatic rescue, playing out slowly, bit by bit; and in the end somehow pulling off what seemed impossible and giving the world a moment of much-needed happiness.

"In my opinion, the whole world is the hero," said Governor Narongsak.

At a time when the news cycle was so often full of violence, meanness, and stupidity, here was something we could all get behind. Was there a single person in the world hoping the boys *wouldn't* get out? For once, we were all on one side, united in hope. We were all on Team Wild Boars. And for just a moment, when those boys and their coach emerged from the cave, it felt like we'd all won.

AFTER
THE CAVE

25

SENDING THE WILD BOARS HOME

After the dramatic rescue, the thirteen members of the Wild Boars were confined to the quarantine ward at Prachanukroh Hospital in Chiang Rai. It was a large, sterile room, with beds lined up against two walls, facing each other. For the first day, the boys' families were able only to wave at them from behind a glass window: after so long in the cave, doctors were worried the boys and Coach Ek would be vulnerable to infections.

The parents wept as they looked at their sons. Young Titan asked a nurse to go and "tell my mom not to cry."

On the second day, the parents were able to go into the ward, but they had to stay at the foot of the beds. No physical contact was allowed. It was only toward the end of day three of the boys' return to the world that the parents were finally allowed to hug their children.

"I was so happy to have him back," said Sak, about his son Biw. "It's like everyone says: it's like winning the lottery."

The Thai government released video of each of the boys introducing themselves, thanking their rescuers, and naming the food they most wanted to eat. Most of the Wild Boars craved pork—crispy pork, pork leg, roasted red pork, grilled pork, minced pork. It was clear they'd given the subject considerable thought.

The doctors said that, considering the ordeal they'd been through, their health was remarkably good. Two of the boys had lung infections, and one had a slow heartbeat. Some also had high white blood cell counts—a sign that their bodies were working hard to fight off infection. They were given a weeklong course of antibiotics and kept in the hospital for monitoring. They bounced back quickly.

When they were finally discharged on July 18, it was an emotional scene. Doctors and nurses lined up to bid farewell to the boys, who stopped for high fives and hugs. Each one also paused in front of a video camera to *wai* and say thanks.

Fourteen-year-old Adul once again proved himself to be an eloquent spokesman for the group as he thanked those who had looked after them—and had taken plenty of blood samples:

Hi. Ever since the first day I came here, I have felt all the doctors and nurses have welcomed us with open hearts, since you guys worried about us so much when we were in the cave. I don't know what to say, and now that we're parting ways, I don't know when we will meet again. I want to come back and meet all of you again, but when that will be will be up to fate. I feel that I love all of you. To all doctors, nurses, and everyone, you didn't just puncture my skin, you also punctured my heart. I love you all.

Once they left the hospital, the Wild Boars were taken to a press conference. It was the triumphant moment the world had waited for—a chance to see the twelve boys and their coach out of the hospital, talking about their ordeal.

The event was held at a local government hall on Wednesday, July 18. In front of the stage, a miniature soccer field had been installed, complete with three-foot-high goals and several soccer balls. A banner on the back wall read in Thai: "Sending the Wild Boars Home."

The media buildup was huge. We arrived three hours before the start time, and soon afterward all likely spots for tripods had been taken. A long line snaked out from the front door as journalists and camera crews waited to register. About thirty photographers and videographers hovered around a side door, hoping to get a good shot of the team arriving.

Eventually the boys emerged from around a corner, all dressed in white-and-green soccer jerseys. They smiled and *wai*'d at the crowd.

"*Nong, nong, nong!*" shouted the photographers, trying to get the boys to look their way as they entered the hall.

The team shuffled in and play-acted for the crowd and cameras, kicking the soccer balls around on the tiny field before taking their place on the stage on two long bench seats. The director of the hospital and two psychologists joined the team onstage. So did the four brave Thais who had stayed with the boys—Dr. Pak and the three SEALs, semi-disguised in surgical masks and sunglasses to protect their identities.

The boys looked surprisingly healthy. Each had regained about six pounds in the week or so since the rescue, and they'd had fresh haircuts as well. The session was hosted by a well-known media personality and broadcast live on Thai television, with all questions prescreened and asked by a moderator.

The team went through some key moments of their ordeal—why they went to the cave, how they survived, and what it was like being found by the British divers.

"My brain was getting slow, as we'd been stuck for ten days. The subjects of math and English were all gone," said Adul modestly.

Dr. Pak and the SEALs talked about how they'd kept the boys' spirits up and about the food they had discussed.

"Many of them had promised me and the SEALs team that they will bring us some exotic food, like Northern-style sausage made from snake meat, and Burmese food," said Dr. Pak.

"I already had almost everything I wanted to eat—bread with chocolate and *kao pad krapao* [crispy pork stir-fried with basil]," said Tern.

"I got what I wanted," said little Mark. "Congee!"

The boys apologized to their parents for not telling them they were going to the cave.

"I would also like to apologize and tell them, 'I love you.' I understand the value of not being truthful to our parents, as it could later make them disappointed," said Adul.

The psychologists reported that all thirteen were doing well mentally, but were vulnerable to post-traumatic stress disorder (PTSD). The new governor of Chiang Rai, Prachon Pratsakul, urged the media and public to leave them alone and let them get back to their normal lives.

The team was asked about the death of Saman Gunan. The boys and Coach Ek had found out about his death only after they'd spent several days in the hospital, and it had hit them hard—knowing their misadventure had cost a man his life.

"I feel sorry and also impressed by Ja Sam, that he gave up his life to protect the Wild Boar children. All thirteen of us got out and will live happy and normal lives," said Coach Ek.

Someone had drawn a lovely pencil sketch of Sergeant Sam, and the team had all signed a message on it. They wanted to present the framed portrait to his widow. Titan stood up to read one of the messages: "My condolences. May you rest in peace, and thank you for sacrificing both body and mind. My deepest condolences to the family of Sergeant. I'd like to thank you, Sergeant, and your family. I hope that you rest in peace."

As Titan turned his back to the audience to read this heartfelt message, his hand unconsciously reached behind and started to adjust his underwear. The crowd tried desperately not to laugh as his hand stayed back there, reorganizing his inner layer, trying to get comfortable in his new clothes.

The boys were asked what they wanted to be when they grew up. Almost all said they wanted to be soccer players. Some wanted to be soccer players *and* Navy SEALs.

Asked if they'd learned anything from the ordeal, Adul said he had. "Having been given this chance, I will live my life more carefully and live it to the fullest."

Home was a long time coming for the boys of the Wild Boars Academy Football Club. There were the ten days trapped with no food. Then six more days before the rescues even started. And even once they were free, they were quarantined for another ten days.

"I am very happy to be home. I was finally able to sleep well last night," said Coach Ek, who, as the only adult, had borne the extra burden of guilt about taking the team to the cave.

After a few days' rest, the boys were keen to get back to school and see their friends.

But for Note, Tee, and Adul, something was weird. They'd just been through an amazing ordeal, one that had captivated the world—but now their schoolmates were pretending it hadn't happened. It was surreal.

"I was confused why nobody came to ask me anything about the cave. But the principal had told them not to," said Adul.

Before long, things started to return to some kind of normal.

"I was very happy that my friends welcomed me back and organized a birthday party for me," said Dom.

Dom would soon have more than four hundred thousand followers on his Instagram account. It was something all the boys would have to get used to, now that they were the famous Wild Boars.

The fact that four of those stuck in the cave were stateless shone a spotlight on the issue. While five hundred thousand people were officially registered as stateless in Thailand, the real number is thought to be as high as three and a half million. Being stateless means dealing with restrictions on where they can go (usually not outside the province's border) and their ability to get a job. Stateless people can't legally marry or get a loan.

The three stateless boys—Mark, Tee, and Adul—were able to go to school and access basic health care. Coach Ek was pretty much on his own, though. The fact that he'd previously applied for a work permit—something only foreigners needed—made it even trickier.

Initially, the new governor of Chiang Rai said the Wild Boars wouldn't be given any special treatment when it came to their citizenship applications: theirs would be processed just like any others.

A few weeks later, though, there was some good news. The Mae Sai district chief, Somsak Kanakham—who had shown an interest in helping the stateless soccer players even before their cave ordeal—had approved their applications. The boys were eligible, he said, because they could prove they had been born in Thailand. Coach Ek was also given papers as an "award of merit." They received their Thai ID cards in August.

They had been embraced by the Thai public; now they truly belonged.

26
BITTERSWEET

On Saturday, July 14, a sea of black-clad mourners gathered around an elaborate cremation platform. It was the sort of send-off usually reserved for high-ranking officials or royals, but this was a funeral for a hero, a former soldier who lost his life rescuing others. Saman Gunan's coffin had been brought back by military escort to his hometown of Roi Et, in the northeast of Thailand. His body was taken to a temple and laid out for friends and family to pay their last respects. In the Thai tradition, they took little silver cups of water and poured the contents over the dead man's hand, into a bowl of flowers. It took several days to construct Saman's crematorium, which looked a bit like a small temple, decorated with garlands of white and yellow flowers.

The king sent his top man, Privy Councilor General Surayud Chulanont, to represent the palace at the service. Narongsak Os-ottanakorn, the rescue commander, attended on behalf of the Wild Boars, who were still in the hospital at the time. Rows of soldiers stood at attention, near officials in white uniforms and black armbands.

Saman's widow was there, her eyes red from crying. In a later interview with the BBC, she talked about her pride and grief.

"I really loved him," said Waleeporn Gunan. "Every day before he left for work we said we loved each other. At midday we'd text to see if the other had had lunch.

"Saman once said, 'We never know when we will die, we can't control that, so we need to cherish every day.' If you ask me if I'm sad, it's like I died but I'm still alive. But I use my pride to repress my sadness. He's been praised as a hero because of who he was. He loved helping others, doing charity work, getting things done. So I use pride to help deal with my sorrow."

She absolved the Wild Boars team of responsibility: "I want to tell the boys, please don't blame yourselves."

And she told the BBC what she would like to say to Saman if she could.

"I want to tell you, honey, 'You are the hero in my heart, you always were and always will be.'"

Saman's father wore heavy black sunglasses as he sat at the funeral with a framed portrait of his son on his lap.

"I am very proud, but I am very sad, too, because I've lost my beloved son," said Wichai Gunan. "May you rest in peace, rest well. Daddy loves you."

Ryan Blair and other friends in the adventure-sports world mourned the loss of a gifted athlete and warm-spirited teammate. They tried to think of the good times they'd shared.

"One of my fondest memories was when we were celebrating our team win and watching the live music entertainment at the 2012 River Kwai Trophy awards ceremony," Ryan wrote in a Facebook tribute.

> Saman got so excited as they were playing Isaan music from his home region. He all of a sudden ran up onstage and took the instrument [a Thai pan flute] and started jamming with the band. He then proceeded to rip his shirt off and started dancing and continued playing.
>
> Saman, you were one of the most unique persons and passionate athletes I have ever raced with or been around. Your whole life and career seemed to be tied to helping others—national service, bodyguard work, special SEAL missions when called, security at the airport, youth programs in Kanchanaburi. I know you would have wanted to be the first person to help those kids in the cave and, I'm sure, jumped in as soon as you got the chance, no matter what the risks. You gave your life for the ultimate sacrifice, helping others, and you really are a true hero.

Saman Gunan was posthumously promoted to the rank of lieutenant commander and awarded the royal decoration of Knight Grand Cross (first class) of the Most Exalted Order of the White Elephant. In a final honor, the king sent a "royal flame" to light the pyre.

The news of Saman Gunan's death had touched the Wild Boars deeply. They wanted to do something to show their gratitude and, in the Thai style of modern Buddhism, "make merit" (do good deeds) for his soul. They decided to get ordained as novice monks at a temple in Mae Sai.

On July 23, eleven of the boys and Coach Ek entered the

temple. (Adul wasn't there. He was a Christian and had shown his thanks at church, where he played guitar and sang.) It was a rainy day, but they went barefoot. They sat in a row, wearing white clothing, their hands pressed together in the Thai gesture of prayer. They had their heads shaved and then they changed into orange robes.

The team stayed at the temple for thirteen days, meditating, chanting, and learning about Buddhism. On August 5, the boys left the temple, handing back their robes and changing into blue trousers and white T-shirts. But Coach Ek stayed on as a monk for several more weeks. Most evenings, the boys would go to the temple to visit him. It seemed their bond was stronger than ever.

Amid the joy, there would be one more cruel twist to the rescue saga.

Hours after Dr. Richard Harris had played such a pivotal role in saving the boys and Coach Ek, returning them safely to their families, his own father died unexpectedly in Adelaide.

His name was Jim Harris.

"Harry put the mission first . . . now he's having to come to deal with what actually happened overnight," said Andrew Pearce, a colleague at an Adelaide rescue service. "You've given your all and then you find out the sad news about your father, who's your best mate—that's really, really tough."

A few days later, on board an RAAF C-17 on the way back to Australia with Craig Challen and Australian team members from the Department of Foreign Affairs and Trade, Australian Federal Police, and Australian Defence Force, Harry wrote a lengthy post on Facebook. He said it was his first chance to reflect on what had happened in Chiang Rai.

He acknowledged the work of local divers and the British team (whom he dubbed "the awesome foursome") in laying the all-important guideline, without which the rescue would have been impossible. "The efforts and skill of these guys in blazing this trail cannot be underestimated," he wrote. "Following someone else's line is very much easier than finding your own way."

Dr. Harry also gave credit to the many Thai and international volunteers involved in the massive effort, doing everything—providing catering, helping pump water from the cave, finding ways to drill into the cave, and scouring the mountain for alternative access routes.

He then heaped praise on the support divers involved in the rescue, before recognizing the Australian, American, Chinese, and Thai teams for their part in getting the Wild Boars safely out of the cave and to a hospital. The Facebook post was his way of giving credit to everyone involved.

"The part we played," he wrote, "has been made out to be a lot more noble than it actually was, we just consider ourselves lucky to have had some skills that we could contribute to the wonderful outcome."

Selflessly, he did not mention the pain of his father's death in this message to the world.

Australia's prime minister, Malcolm Turnbull, called Dr. Harry and Craig to offer his condolences for Dr. Harry's loss and congratulate them on their heroism.

"No worries," Dr. Harry replied. "The big heroes in this are the children and the four Navy SEALs who were looking after them. They are the toughest blokes and kids I have ever had the privilege to meet."

A few weeks later, far from Thailand, at Government House in Canberra, the leaders from both sides of Australian politics gathered. The governor-general, Sir Peter Cosgrove, was also present. Nine men sat rather stiffly at the front of the room. Two of them wore suits; seven wore formal uniforms. They were to receive bravery medals.

"We think that you were remarkable—skillful, tireless, compassionate, and courageous. Your nation is so proud of you. Today, Australia salutes you," said Governor-General Cosgrove.

Dr. Richard Harris and Craig Challen were presented with the Star of Courage, the second-highest Australian bravery decoration, awarded for "acts of conspicuous courage in circumstances of great peril."

The six Australian Federal Police rescue specialists and a member of the navy received bravery medals. They were: Senior Constable Justin John Bateman, Leading Senior Constable Kelly Craig Boers, Detective Leading Senior Constable Benjamin Walter Cox, First Constable Matthew Peter Fitzgerald, Acting Station Sergeant Robert Michael James, Detective Leading Senior Constable Christopher John Markcrow, and the one man from the defense force, Chief Petty Officer Troy Matthew Eather.

All nine received the Medal of the Order of Australia, too.

Dr. Harry once again shared the glory with the wider team.

"We just went cave diving for a few days and were able to get the kids out. . . . These awards have been completely unexpected, and we're just trying to emphasize how big a part so many people played in this," he said.

But there was some sense of the enormity of what had been accomplished by the international team.

"Cave diving is what we do. That bit didn't require anything special," said Craig. "But what we are not used to is holding these little humans in our hands and their fate completely up to us. What we did at the time made all the difference between them surviving and not."

But when asked about their own roles in the rescue, like Dr. Harry, he played down the honor: "We're just a couple of ordinary blokes with an unusual hobby."

27
HUNTING THE WILD BOARS

Despite the calls from officials to leave the boys alone, some media organizations were desperate for a quick hit. But the way a few news organizations hunted down the Wild Boars left many in the media and wider society deeply uncomfortable.

It was later reported that the American Broadcasting Company (a commercial organization unrelated to the publicly funded Australian Broadcasting Corporation) had eighteen local producers working the night of the Wild Boars' first press conference, posted at the boys' homes. They turned up uninvited to the welcome-home parties, and, in some cases, the families were too polite to refuse. The morning after the press conference, their correspondent, James Longman, showed up at Titan's house bearing a basket of dried bird's-nest soup—a traditional gift for the infirm, but an odd one for an eleven-year-old boy.

The American Broadcasting Company also filmed Night being stripped to his shorts and doused with a bucket of water in a ritual, and Adul in church being hugged and fed pieces of fried chicken. It all made for great TV.

The Thai government reportedly offered the families safehouses, but they preferred to find refuge in the homes of friends and relatives. The attention crowded the boys. When Biw wanted to visit Adul in those first days of freedom, he asked his father if he'd have to climb over the wall of their house to escape the waiting media.

From each of these news agencies, there were no doubt backslapping and hero-grams. But in Thailand, there was a strong backlash.

"The interviews should not have been done at all," said Tawatchai Thaikyo, the deputy permanent secretary of Thailand's Ministry of Justice. "Some questions can trigger fears in the boys, especially questions about medication before the extraction from the cave. Such questions remind them of the traumatic experience they went through and may result in a chronic depression in the future.

"Although the foreign agencies claimed that they received a permission from the boys' parents, it is not right because Thai and foreign journalists were informed of clear guidelines on the coverage. The parents of the boys might not be prepared to cope with what's to come," Tawatchai Thaikyo told the *Bangkok Post*.

Some government officials went even further, threatening legal action under the Child Protection Act. It went nowhere, but it showed the anger they felt toward the journalists who had blatantly ignored requests from doctors and officials.

The situation posed an ethical dilemma for all of us in the media. We all wanted to hear more from the boys and their families, but the request for privacy was a reasonable one. Jum and I decided that we wouldn't push for an interview but would try to let our contacts know we were keen to talk when they were ready.

Jum had been in contact with Sak, Biw's dad, and called him on July 19 (the day after the boys got out of the hospital) to see how he was doing, and to say that we'd be very interested in doing an interview, when the time was right. He said it was too soon for anything on camera, but invited us all for beers on the mountain.

Several fathers of the boys had gathered at a hillside restaurant with a panoramic view of the mountains. Jum, David, and I joined the table of dads and a few of their friends, who had been drawn in as unofficial advisers. Often in Southeast Asia, you "cheers" just about every time you drink, and so it was that night, arms stretched across the table at regular intervals. We'd decided on the way there to avoid asking questions about the boys or the rescue—to keep it light and social, make friends. But we needn't have worried; the rescue was all the fathers could talk about.

Jum translated parts, and I gained a glimpse of the complicated situation into which these families had been thrust. Politics, greed, and opportunities surrounded them, and they discussed how to pick a path through the madness. They talked about the supernatural elements of the story. They were clearly exhausted, but happy. Over and over, we all clinked glasses.

"Have you ever tried ducks' beaks?" Sak asked me.

I had to check the translation a couple of times, thinking back through my exotic eating list.

"No, definitely not," I said.

"Would you like to?"

I had a feeling I was being tested.

"Sure," I said.

Soon, a plate of deep-fried morsels arrived and we tucked in. I watched for the technique: hold the beak and nibble the meat from around the head. They were surprisingly good; like tiny battered drumsticks. We ordered another plate.

As the place began to fill up, a talented female singer took to the stage, her pure voice accompanied by a man on an electric keyboard.

"Can you sing?" asked Sak.

"Yeah, sure," I said, again feeling a test.

He gestured to the stage. Yikes.

"Hmm, I don't know. If I had a guitar I could," I said, hoping to squirm off on a technicality.

The owner, who'd been sitting with us, got up and returned a few minutes later with an acoustic guitar. Damn, now I couldn't back out. My repertoire consisted mostly of downbeat Americana and obscure Australian songs. Not for the first time, I cursed myself for not learning "Hotel California."

Soon I found myself onstage. Black-and-white pictures of Elvis and an old Thai crooner covered the wall behind me. Instead of a seat, there was a retro-style motorcycle to sit on. I introduced myself in my limited Thai and began playing a ballad by Little Feat, "Roll Um Easy." The patrons stopped and listened, no doubt for the novelty rather than the talent. When the song was finished, there was mild applause. I played one more song— the Lucksmiths' "Frisbee"—said thank you, *wai*'d the crowd, and beat a hasty exit, stage left.

I slipped back to the table to a round of "cheers." Had I passed the test? It was hard to tell. The conversation continued, and the adrenaline rush of an impromptu performance subsided. After more snacks and beers, we told the fathers we would leave them be; no doubt they had things to discuss privately. They said to stick around; they'd be leaving soon anyway.

As we walked out to the parking lot, a soft drizzle fell. Sak said we should come and meet his son. We declined, conscious of our efforts to not intrude.

"Just for five minutes," he said.

We didn't refuse a second time and convoyed back to the house.

We met Biw and sat around on woven mats while he told the family some of his incredible story. We let his family ask most of the questions. Per our agreement, I didn't report any of the details Biw shared. Much later, Sak gave his permission to reveal the meeting for this book.

After the rescue and the public press conference, access to the Wild Boars was highly restricted. The boys' families were told by the Thai government not to talk to any media and to let the authorities manage all requests.

Around mid-August, a rumor spread that the Thai government was planning a secret interview session with the Wild Boars, specially arranged for the American Broadcasting Company. It didn't make sense—a few weeks earlier, the Thai government had been talking about charging the American Broadcasting Company and others for violating the Child Protection Act. Now they were rolling out the red carpet for them. What had changed?

The question was not *what* had changed, but *who*. In August, the government's deputy spokesman Major-General Werachon Sukondhapatipak was appointed the head of the Creative Media for Tham Luang Cave Committee.

I raced to the airport to fly to Chiang Rai. If there was a genuine media opportunity, I wanted to be there. And if it was a dodgy deal, I wanted to see that, too. As I pulled up to the departure gate, Major-General Werachon returned my call.

I asked him if he had arranged a deal with the American Broadcasting Company.

"There is a committee to consider the proposal," he replied. "It is government policy, first to protect the children; second, we need to know the storyboard; third, we need to know all of the questions. All of this will be considered. But I cannot tell if it has been granted or not."

"But will there be a secret press conference for the American Broadcasting Company?"

"I cannot say for sure" was the deputy spokesman's response.

I would later find out that a full TV crew had flown from America and that, as we were having this conversation, they were unpacking three vans of lights, tripods, and cameras at a temple in Mae Sai, the same one where Coach Ek spent his years as a monk.

The monks at the temple, just like the families, were expected to comply with the government's wishes. At least one of the families had called the abbot to see if they could decline to participate. The abbot, realistic of the power play involved, said not really.

The main prayer hall had been rigged with lights and cameras, and the American TV crew was waiting in a room inside the building. The public was forbidden to enter the room to pray; a dark-red velvet curtain had been pulled across the front glass doors. At least five police officers and eight soldiers stood guard and did laps of the hillside pagoda on motorbikes.

At 5 p.m. on the dot, two silver vans drove into the temple grounds and pulled up outside the main hall. Some adults got out of the first one and it pulled away. The second van inched forward, the door slid open, and a blur of yellow shirts popped out as the Wild Boars ran out of the van door and into the prayer hall, much like soccer players running out of the tunnel and onto the field.

The families of the boys were surprised to find foreigners inside the temple—they had been told the interview was for the Thai government program *Moving Forward Thailand*, hosted by none other than Major-General Werachon. But that was a ruse.

A female producer from the American Broadcasting Company got out of the passenger door and walked toward the velvet curtains, raising her clenched fists in the air and then hugging a Thai fixer. They'd done it. For the second time, they had got the exclusive interview. Once again, they'd hunted down the Wild Boars.

The group interview ran the following morning on the network's high-ratings breakfast show. It looked fantastic, with soft golden lighting illuminating a Buddha statue and a portrait of the king in the background. Multiple cameras covered different angles. The content was almost exactly the same as the previous public press conference, which made sense considering that the questions had again been vetted.

The psychologists had agreed to a forty-five-minute interview with the Wild Boars. But in the end, the filming took more than four hours, albeit with breaks. The families left late in the evening, tired and angry. The boys had smiled and laughed good-naturedly through it, but had been bored.

Major-General Werachon's fuzziness on the phone that morning about whether there was an interview or not had apparently cleared up as the day went on. He personally escorted the TV crew to the provincial government meeting and later translated correspondent James Longman's questions during the taping. A photo posted on social media showed the boys, their coach, and the TV crew. On the edge stood Major-General Werachon, his arm around one of the boys. (Major-General Werachon ignored requests to be interviewed for this book.)

"The interview caused an uproar among local and foreign media which felt the Thai government granted special privilege to the American TV while discouraging others from talking to the thirteen Tham Luang survivors," wrote the state broadcaster Thai PBS a few days later.

Werachon put the whole thing down to a "communication misunderstanding."

"He also dismissed a suggestion that ABC [American Broadcasting Company] News had paid for the right to interview the boys and their coach," stated the Thai PBS article. (The American Broadcasting Company also denied paying money to secure the interview.) "Some parents doubted why their boys were interviewed because they were informed that it would be only an informal talk between an ABC News reporter and the boys."

Unfortunately, that was not the only ethically questionable incident involving those who were supposed to be protecting the Wild Boars.

On September 7, Erik and Mikko went to a fancy Bangkok shopping mall and stood at the edge of the crowd, waiting like everyone else for the boys and Coach Ek to appear onstage. Even though they had helped rescue the boys, they had never actually met them. For those three urgent days, the boys were simply "packages," precious blurs of wet suits and face masks and bubbles. The Koh Tao divers were heroes, but here they were, fanboying like the rest of us in the audience.

The boys sat on two rows of high stools, Titan and Mark in the front for maximum cuteness. To the right of the stage, Coach Ek sat cross-legged, his fresh orange robes almost neon against the black leather chair.

A Q&A got under way, hosted by Major-General Werachon. There was the sense we were being given a very limited glimpse into a private world. The same prescreened questions received more or less the same answers as at the Mae Sai press conference and the American Broadcasting Company interview. Being teenagers, they couldn't always hide their boredom, and on this day, four of them in the back row occasionally whispered to each other from the corners of their mouths and stifled giggles.

They took turns answering. What food did they crave? What did they want to be when they grew up? By now, they had it by rote. Adul was still the designated spokesman, but his voice was becoming raspy. The connection between the boys and Coach Ek was immediately apparent; warm and respectful.

The Q&A ended and the team was led to a nearby display, created by the government to tell the story of the cave rescue. It was excellent, explaining the equipment and techniques used to pull off the daring mission. (Rather strangely, though, an information plaque about Tham Luang described it as representing the "vagina" of the mythical Princess Nang Non in the folk story. Which was odd, since the cave was located about where her left ear should have been.) There was a full-face mask and one of the army-green rescue stretchers on which the boys had been carefully carried through the cave. Visitors could sip tiny plastic cups of the energy gel the boys had first been given. A surprise crowd favorite was the foil space blankets, with kids eager to wrap themselves up and have their photo taken on a fake rock.

The centerpiece was a room-size replica of a cave. As the Wild Boars toured the display, their minders forgot all about protecting the boys' mental well-being. They were ushered into the "cave," crouching to fit into the small space and duck-walking through the darkness, as TV cameras jostled for a shot. If there was ever a trigger for PTSD, it was this—and they'd just been guided into it by the government.

The country's top mental-health specialist said that luckily the stunt didn't seem to affect the boys but was still wildly in-appropriate.

"They are not dolls that anyone can do whatever they want [to]," said Dr. Yongyuth Wongpiromsan, head of Thailand's Department of Mental Health, according to BBC Thai.

Adul was asked about this incident at a later public event. After a moment of coaching, he said they had wanted to go in. Privately, however, several of the boys told me the opposite: they had not wanted to go inside that fake cave, and they did not enjoy the experience.

28
CONTROVERSY

In the latter stages of the rescue, billionaire technology guru Elon Musk offered to help. Best known for his eco-cars, the inventor was also trying to pioneer commercial space travel through his company SpaceX. The Thai public had been enthralled that Musk was getting involved, imagining a dramatic space-age solution to their problem.

At Musk's order, a group of his SpaceX engineers went to work on two ideas. One was a mini-submarine, or pod, that the boys could lie inside. The other was an inflatable tube that they could walk through.

The engineers arrived on-site after the boys had been found. They were clearly brilliant people—"geniuses," according to engineer Suttisak Soralump, who met them. They tested the inflatable tube at a local canal, but, after talking to the SEALs about conditions in the cave, they decided it wouldn't work inside the jagged tunnels of Tham Luang.

That left the pod. It was a six-foot-long silver tube named, of course, *The Wild Boar*. It looked something like a miniature rocket, which was not surprising considering who had built it. On the first day of the rescue, Musk released a video of it being tested in a swimming pool, and on the second day of the rescue, he personally delivered it to Thailand. He met briefly with engineers at Ban Chong temple, then set out for the cave. The pod was left behind; Governor Narongsak had already politely declined its use, saying it wouldn't work. By then, eight boys had already been brought out of the cave alive. They would stick with the diving plan.

Access to the cave was extremely tight during those days, but it was around 10 p.m. when Musk arrived, and the day's operation was over, so he was allowed to enter. According to a witness, the billionaire inventor arrived at the cave and promptly waded into the water until it was up to his neck.

Elon Musk's erratic behavior didn't end with his sudden plunge into the waters of Tham Luang.

He took to social media to attack Governor Narongsak, claiming he wasn't the real commander of the rescue, and citing another Thai man who had been helping advise SpaceX about their projects.

Then things really got nasty.

Vern Unsworth was asked by CNN if he thought the minisub would have worked. Vern was smiling, but his language was colorful.

"Stick his submarine where it hurts," he said. "It just had absolutely no chance of working. He had no conception of what the cave passage was like. The submarine was about five foot six [inches] long, rigid, so it wouldn't have gone around corners or around any obstacles. It wouldn't have made the first fifty meters [about 165 feet] into the cave, from the dive start point. Just a PR stunt."

Elon Musk reacted furiously, tweeting this response: "We will make one [video] of the mini-sub-pod going all the way to Cave 5 no problem. Sorry pedo guy, you really did ask for it."

The tweet was later deleted. Musk offered absolutely no evidence to back his "pedo" claim. Chiang Rai police said no charges or complaints had ever been made against Vern.

In the following days, stocks for the billionaire's main company, Tesla, nosedived, the market shocked at the outburst and concerned about what it meant for Musk's mental stability.

A few days later, Musk took to Twitter again, this time to apologize. He said he'd "spoken in anger after Mr. Unsworth said several untruths & suggested I engage in a sexual act with the mini-sub, which had been built as an act of kindness & according to specifications from the dive team leader."

A lawyer acting on behalf of Vern contacted Musk, suggesting he get in contact to avoid a court case. But the tech boss obviously didn't get the memo. Just when the whole sorry spat had almost been forgotten, Musk let fly again.

In emails to a BuzzFeed reporter in early September, Musk accused Vern of moving to Thailand to marry a twelve-year-old child bride. Once again, the American offered no evidence to back the scandalous claim. The accusation was made all the more bizarre considering that Vern's partner, Tik, was in her forties and had been with him for seven years. Musk had meant the email to be off the record, but the reporter had not agreed to the condition in advance—as is customary—and so published it.

At the time of writing, legal action was pending.

29

APPEASING THE SLEEPING LADY

The nauseating smell of overripe pig flesh wafted through the air, mixing with incense from joss sticks. Each subtle shift in the breeze would reveal one or the other winning the olfactory battle. Animism and Buddhism swirled and blended together, as they so often do in the spiritual lives of Thais.

For some outsiders, it was a strange offering.

Pigs' heads after the rescue of thirteen Wild Boars?

But the long table was also set with chicken, fish, and beautifully decorated floral arrangements in green, white, and yellow—gifts to appease the sleeping princess spirit of the mountain, who some Thais believed had trapped the Wild Boars. A portrait of Saman Gunan in a red beret took a place of honor at one end of the table, shaded by a parasol and surrounded by more flowers.

The ceremony was held on July 16 at the staging area outside the cave entrance. Where SEALs once filled their silver air tanks, now VIP guests, most of them in military uniforms, sat on plastic chairs. Governor Narongsak was guest of honor. Across the dirt road were thousands of volunteers in yellow shirts and blue caps. The boys were still in the hospital but their families were there, dressed in white; they had their own canopy behind the table of pigs' heads, with no line of sight to the spectacle that was about to unfold.

Drums were beaten, conch shells were blown. Male fire-breathers whirled between the VIPs and pigs' heads, exhaling huge flames. Young women in white satin dresses and golden headdresses circled around like Sirens, gracefully throwing flowers into the air.

Governor Narongsak lit four candles on a wooden stand, a summons to the spirits in all four directions of the compass. An elderly man began a long chant of Buddhist prayers.

As the chanting dragged on, I walked off to survey some of the areas that had been off-limits while the operation was under way. I was curious to see inside the building where the coordinators had been throughout the ordeal—the war room.

It had seen better days, with its faded poster and broken cave model. It was hard to believe this was the nerve center for the biggest rescue operation in living memory.

Farther down the hill, where I'd once washed my boots in the blue-pipe fountain, the generator trucks were gone and the area was open. Thais had placed little piles of offerings—food, sweets, and incense sticks—on the soil. It looked like a miniature graveyard, but it was something close to the opposite.

The lower entrance to the cave was now guarded by police. Behind them, a brand-new wire fence reached almost ten feet into the air. Attached to the barbed wire was a sign that said

"DANGER" in English, and in Thai, "Beware of high-voltage electricity." CCTV cameras had also been installed.

The angry princess had been ringed by a modern protective shield. Tham Luang would be closed until January, well after the end of the rainy season.

Behind the tall green fence and the security cameras, the cave remained off-limits. It wasn't just because the authorities wanted to avoid anyone else getting trapped. When the pump broke in Chamber 3 and the monsoon rains sealed the cave, hundreds of thousands of dollars' worth of equipment was left inside. Scuba tanks and regulators, water pumps, generators—all sorts of gear had been lost to the waters. Although much of it would be irreparably damaged, some of it might be recoverable when the rainy season ended.

It's hard to say, exactly, what it is that brought the raging floodwaters inside Tham Luang under control.

The man who knows the cave so well, Vern Unsworth, believes the pumping did little except to clear the way to Chamber 3. He thinks the diverting of the creeks on top of the mountain probably helped most. He says it's a shame the pond at Khun Nam Nang Non was dug up and destroyed so the water from Saitong Cave had somewhere to flow. The Thai government plans to rehabilitate the area within months.

Thanet agrees the groundwater pumping probably only had a "small significance" to the outcome, but these judgments are easy in hindsight. At the time, with lives on the line and so many uncertainties, everything was worth a try. Like Vern, he thinks stopping the flow of the creeks was probably more crucial to lowering the water level inside Tham Luang.

That said, the pumping was impressive. Thanet has calculated a rough estimate of the water that was removed, using the capacity of the pumps and the time they ran. About 502,000 cubic yards was drained from inside Tham Luang (from the sumps between the entrance and Chamber 3) and a further 73,000 cubic yards was pumped out of the groundwater at the front of the cave. Over at Saitong Cave, about 196,000 cubic yards came out of the cave, while a staggering 2,711,000 cubic yards was drained from the aquifer below. All told, that's more than 1,000 Olympic-size swimming pools.

The owners of the "dragon pumps" were cheered as heroes as they drove their rigs out of town after the rescues, people spontaneously lining the streets to see the 59-foot-long contraptions go by.

If they had kept the pumps working in the shrimp ponds, each one could have been earning $45 an hour, but they had forsaken that income to be part of something greater.

"Our hearts drew us here. Twenty of us leave today. I'm happy that they [the Wild Boars] are safe. . . . I'm proud we helped the kids," said Thawatchai Fuengkachorn, leader of the team.

The baby wild boar trotted around, ferreted among the leaves with its snout, and trotted on. His name was Bon: in Thai, the word for soccer is pronounced "footbon." Bon had been brought to the cave as a symbolic offering during the rescue and had since become something of a mascot for Tham Luang.

He was fed by construction workers, who were laying the foundations for a museum, located about where we had squelched around in the press tent a few weeks earlier. The museum would be paid for by national artist and Chiang Rai resident Chalermchai Kositpipat. A large statue of Saman Gunan would stand out front, and the museum would showcase the unity and daring that helped pull off the rescue.

For some locals, all the news coverage about the science of the rescue did little to dull their interpretations of events. For the seventy-nine-year-old former village chief and keeper of local legends Grandfather Boonma Kabjainai, there was a spiritual explanation for the whole affair. He believed the princess who haunted the mountain had trapped the boys in order to lure in soldiers.

"She doesn't want normal people, she only wants soldiers," said Grandfather Boonma.

The tragic death of Saman Gunan fitted neatly into his story—a former soldier's life paid as a penance for the princess, revenge for the soldiers who had killed her lover.

"I think there will be no more [disappearances]," he said. "She got her soldier already."

But despite the dark tale, Grandfather Boonma thought there was hope for the vengeful spirit. With all the rituals and prayers offered up by the boys, their parents, local officials, monks, and shamans, he thought that maybe—just maybe—the ghost of the angry princess might be sated, ready to leave the restless spirit world and be reincarnated.

"Perhaps Nang Non is ready to be reborn, as a human."

EPILOGUE

In the days and weeks that followed their rescue, life was a bit strange for the Wild Boars. It took some time for them to realize just what a global phenomenon they'd become while sitting on that muddy ledge. Life outside was complicated. Their families were pulled this way and that by the government, by media, by movie producers, by money, and by their own efforts to deal with their newfound fame.

They were dutiful boys and went along with the rituals and ceremonies and endless photos with good grace. They thanked their rescuers over and over for saving them, and the world for sending hope and love. They pledged to be good citizens and make the most of the lives they so nearly lost.

Slowly, some sense of normality began to return. At school, the boys faced the unglamorous reality of catching up with the curriculum. Until they were back on track with their school work, there would be no soccer. Those were the rules set by their parents.

After school, they were almost always together. Inside the cave, they'd made a pact to support each other, and that transferred to the outside world. Many afternoons were spent riding or running up the hill together to the temple to see Coach Ek. Lots of people came to see Coach Ek, wanting to get blessed by this celebrity monk. When the boys were ordained as novices, it was the same for them. Many people donated money to them. They pooled the cash and bought a bike for Adul, the one member of their tight-knit group who didn't have one. It was an act of generosity and mateship that said much about these boys.

They were average kids who'd had an extraordinary misadventure. Their lives were no more special than any others, but for a few weeks they had become the most worried-over boys in the world, and their survival became an international priority.

And they had survived. Against all odds, they had defied the fears of even their rescuers and somehow made it out alive. By doing so, they had brought the most profound feelings of relief and happiness to millions of people who'd never met them. Their journey into the darkness, so close to death, had managed to unite a divided world, just for a moment.

Now they would have to try to get on with their lives. They were still the same good kids they were when they stepped into the cave, but their ordeal had opened their minds and hearts and opportunities.

They were young, full of talent, full of dreams.

There would be more adventures.

ACKNOWLEDGMENTS

I have been fortunate to work with some of the best field producers and researchers in Thailand. They each played different roles, and each was crucial.

Jum (Supattra Vimonsuknopparat) is the ABC Bangkok bureau's producer. In her spare time and even while on holiday, Jum was working behind the scenes (often without me even knowing it) to arrange interviews or search for fresh information. Jum laid the foundation for whom I should talk to for this book and helped fact-check the draft.

Nat (Nat Sumon) helped me get many of the key interviews that made this book. She spent two weeks in Chiang Rai guiding me to wonderful interviews and translating brilliantly. Nat was part of the most dramatic quests for interviews, and she drove me home when I just *had* to drink all that moonshine!

Based in Chiang Mai, Am (Am Puchara Sandford) was on the scene early at Tham Luang. Her natural ease with people made her one of the most trusted journalists on-site for the families. Her timely advice led me to key interviews.

Tin (Boontin Posayanukul) arranged several interviews and attended conferences about the rescue, which yielded good information. He did long translations, and much of that work has ended up in the book.

Katie (Kampirada Hongpetrasmi) led me to one of the strangest interviews of the book, exploring the ghostly dreams that brought Kruba Boonchum to the mountain. Unfortunately, the "dark spirit" didn't help us win the lottery.

Reuters correspondent Panu (Panu Wongcha-um) was one of the hardest-working men on the mountain during the search and rescue. He contributed photographs and fact-checked the draft manuscript.

Rachel Dennis did an incredible job of editing my hastily written first draft. My thanks to Mary Rennie at HarperCollins Australia for first proposing the book and seeing it through, and to Madeleine James (also at HarperCollins Australia) for her work on the photographs and maps.

During my three weeks at Tham Luang, David Leland endured long hours that few camera operators would have put up with: a consummate professional.

I was joined in the mud by another team from the ABC; my thanks to these wonderful colleagues: Anne Barker (reporter), Billy Cooper (cameraman), Phil Hemmingway (cameraman), and Angel (fixer). Brant Cummings arrived at Tham Luang late in the story, to replace Billy, and contributed several photographs for the book.

Thanks to Mark Willacy, Lucy Carter, Mat Marsic, and Rob Mackay, the *Four Corners* team who quickly produced an excellent documentary.

Upsorn Yeo and Khun Tu (Channarong Apicharttham) kept the bureau going while I was on leave writing.

Thanks to Julia Hu in Australia and Pun (Chaninthorn Pitak-wararat) in Thailand for translating interviews with the Chinese team, and to my dad, Ian Cochrane, for the literary references. Dr. Michael Sheridan generously checked some of the medical references.

I'd like to thank Michael Hayes, who gave me my start in journalism at the *Phnom Penh Post*. His essential rules of reporting and ongoing friendship have had a lasting impact.

Breeze (Parveena Thakrainate) always knew just when to give me space and when to turn up with delicious Thai food. So much of what I know about Thailand is because of you. My love and thanks.

A huge thanks to my friends Aaron and Clara for their constant encouragement and for being so understanding when I spent most of our beach holiday inside typing. Also, to their son Marley for trying to eat pumpkin soup with his fingers, which is how the writing felt some days.

Love and thanks to my mum, Pam; brother, Dale; and sister, Caitlin, for always being there for me.

Phoebe Bridgers's album *Stranger in the Alps* provided the soundtrack to my time in Mae Sai and while writing this book.

My thanks to everyone who generously gave their time for interviews. Many people were hounded by the media, and I appreciate those who took the time to share their perspectives with me.

Finally, to the boys and Coach Ek. The thought of what they went through in that cave inspired me to work harder and be thankful for the opportunity.

ABOUT THE AUTHOR

Liam Cochrane is the Australian Broadcasting Corporation's Southeast Asia correspondent, based in Bangkok. He spent more than two weeks in Mae Sai covering the cave rescue, one of those weeks stationed outside the cave entrance in the mud. Liam began his career in journalism in Cambodia in 2004, as a reporter, then managing editor of the *Phnom Penh Post*. He freelanced in Nepal for two years and returned to Melbourne to host *Connect Asia* on ABC Radio Australia. Before Bangkok, he was posted to Port Moresby, considered the ABC's toughest correspondent position. He was the only foreign reporter on Manus Island when Australia's asylum seeker detention center was attacked in 2014.